Interpretation

By

Graphic Design Basics
for Heritage Interpreters

Paul Caputo   Shea Lewis   Lisa Brochu

■ On the cover:
Rhododendron
in Hamarikyu
Garden, Tokyo
(Paul Caputo);
interpretive
sign at Parkin
Archeological
State Park in
Arkansas (Shea
Lewis); and
management sign
in Twin Lakes,
Colorado (Paul
Caputo).

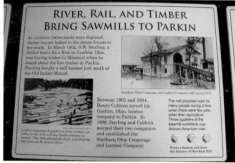

RIVER, RAIL, AND TIMBER
BRING SAWMILLS TO PARKIN

interpPress

Copyright © 2008 Paul Caputo, Shea Lewis, and Lisa Brochu
ISBN-10: 1–879931–25–7
ISBN-13: 978–1–879931–25–1

NATIONAL ASSOCIATION FOR
INTERPRETATION

The National Association for Interpretation is a private
nonprofit [501(c)3] organization and professional association.
NAI's mission is: "Inspiring leadership and excellence to
advance natural and cultural interpretation as a profession."
For information, visit www.interpnet.com.

 Printed on recycled paper.

For Sheila, the blue to my orange.

—*PC*

For Sebrena, my muse whose love strengthens me.

—*SL*

For Tim, my constant inspiration.

—*LB*

Contents

Acknowledgments vii

Foreword by Jim Covel ix

Introduction 1

1 Understanding the Basics 3

2 Planning the Message 7

3 The Design Process 19

4 Elements of Design 25

5 Technical Specifications 53

6 Special Considerations for Specific Applications 65

7 Making the Collaborative Process Work 81

8 Resources 97

Glossary 107

Index 115

Acknowledgments

The authors thank the following individuals. Donna Richardson, Vice President for Programs on the National Association for Interpretation's Board of Directors, helped make this book a reality. Mary Ann Bonnell, Russell Dickerson, Jamie King, Tim Merriman, and Roger Riolo graciously shared their considerable artistic talents, providing some of the photographs and illustrations that appear in this text. Thanks also to Boulder County Parks and Open Space and Condit Exhibits for use of materials related to the Stroh/Dickens Barn. Kathy Caputo, Russell Dickerson, and Katie Roberts took time to offer their expert advice on artistic and technical content of the book. Elizabeth Meyers copyedited the final manuscript and Lynda Stannard of Thistle Index generated the book's index.

Foreword

In this "information age," we have access to an unprecedented amount of information. However it can easily feel like we are being bombarded by information coming from all angles at an excessive rate. As a result, we are becoming sophisticated consumers of information, developing more and more filters to prevent overload. Only the most attractive, most engaging, and most accessible information is going to get past our filters.

To paraphrase Freeman Tilden, information is not interpretation—interpretation is much more. So by using interpretive methods and principles to communicate important content, we're already making it more engaging and appealing for its intellectual and emotional stimulation. But that interpretive treatment of the content goes beyond the mere words; it has to apply to the presentation as well. In print media, this means the overall layout and design, as well as the language itself, must speak clearly to the audience.

Many interpreters have traditionally been trained in the accurate and effective presentation of content through the spoken and written word. We've often had to rely on people trained in other disciplines— graphic arts, typography, design—to provide the presentation of interpretive messages in brochures, exhibit labels, websites, and other visual media. *Interpretation By Design* brings these heretofore separate disciplines into a unified approach to effective interpretation with visual media. It can help traditional interpreters to use graphic design principles and practices to improve his or her own projects or work more effectively with designers.

Simply put, the goal of interpretation is to forge intellectual and emotional connections with our audience. *Interpretation By Design* provides new and powerful tools to help us achieve this goal.

Jim Covel
President
National Association for Interpretation
August 2008

Introduction

In 2003, Shea Lewis, superintendent of Parkin Archeological State Park in Arkansas, called Paul Caputo, the new art director for the National Association for Interpretation (NAI), and suggested that they submit a proposal to present a concurrent session at that year's NAI National Workshop in Sparks, Nevada. The session would address the growing need for basic training in graphic design for interpreters who had been asked to create brochures, newsletters, websites, and other nonpersonal media, but who had little or no background in design. The proposal stressed that the session would not only address interpretive principles and the building blocks of graphic design, but how to use those interpretive principles to make meaningful design decisions. Just as frontline interpretation is thematic, so, too, should every decision about type, color, and composition in graphic design be founded in the larger meaning of an overriding message.

Meanwhile, NAI Associate Director Lisa Brochu, already a leader in the field with several decades of experience as an interpreter, consultant, and author or co-author of four books on heritage interpretation, was building NAI's certification and training programs to introduce and reinforce interpretive principles and procedures to thousands of individuals practicing in the field.

Shea and Paul presented "Meeting in the Middle: Combining Elements of Interpretation and Graphic Design" for the first time on November 13, 2003, in Sparks, Nevada, at the NAI National Workshop. More than 100 people crowded into the room for the hour-long session—not so much an indication of their appreciation for Shea's and Paul's wit and charm, but of the sincere need for training in this area. Since then, Shea and Paul have presented "Meeting in the Middle" as a concurrent session or all-day preworkshop at NAI National Workshops in Grand Rapids, Michigan; Mobile, Alabama; Albuquerque, New Mexico; Wichita, Kansas; and Portland, Oregon. Paul has presented the session at NAI International Conferences in San Juan, Puerto Rico; Vancouver, Canada; and

Sokcho, South Korea; and at NAI regional workshops in North Bend, Washington; Dubuque, Iowa; Dickinson, North Dakota; Tulsa, Oklahoma; and Fort Collins, Colorado. Shea presented the session at Fall Creek Falls State Park in Tennessee. Paul and Lisa have presented "Interpretation By Design," a two-day course that derives from NAI's Certified Heritage Interpreter curriculum, in Lewes, Delaware, and Fort Collins, Colorado.

As solid attendance at these sessions continued over the years, it became increasingly clear that budget constraints and staff cutbacks at interpretive sites were creating a new role for frontline interpreters: the unprepared designer—the interpreter who has no training in the principles of graphic design, but who is asked to produce nonpersonal media because he or she is familiar with interpretation and knows how to work a computer and some software.

This book represents the accumulated experience and knowledge of three professionals with very different backgrounds and careers. Paul's experience in visual communications is a foundation for sound graphic design principles. Shea's background with Arkansas State Parks brings the essential perspective of the frontline interpreter and interpretive manager. And Lisa's knowledge of interpretive principles and the history and traditions of the field places the tips and techniques contained within in the context of the larger interpretive picture.

More importantly, this text reflects the belief that the design and production of nonpersonal interpretive media should be thoughtfully planned. Even the smallest decision about a font, color, or other design element should be meaningful, relate to a larger message, and help build the identity of a site or organization.

Paul Caputo
Shea Lewis
Lisa Brochu

August 2008

■ Opposite page: Interpretive exhibit at the Chesapeake Bay Maritime Museum in St. Michaels, Maryland.

Canning

Shuckin

LISA BROCHU

Definition of Interpretation

Although interpretation has been around since people began communicating, it wasn't until the 21st century that the National Association for Interpretation defined the term.

> Interpretation is a mission-based communication process that forges emotional and intellectual connections between the interests of the audience and the meanings inherent in the resource.

Interpretation can be personal, in which case an interpreter communicates a message directly to the public by taking visitors on a guided tour, presenting a campfire program, or chatting informally with a group on the deck of a cruise ship. Personal interpretation can take place in any setting on any subject, but requires a person to deliver a message. It is sometimes referred to as "active" interpretation.

Interpretation can also be nonpersonal, using other media

Understanding the Basics

such as publications, exhibits, signs, sculptures, food service, or sales items to communicate the message. Nonpersonal interpretation, by definition, does not require an interpreter to be present to deliver a message. This type of interpretation is sometimes referred to as "passive" interpretation.

Principles of Interpretation

Freeman Tilden is often called the "father of interpretation." Ironically, Tilden was not an interpreter, but a journalist and playwright. In the 1950s, the National Park Service asked Tilden to examine the interface between park rangers and the public. He visited a number of national parks and studied the communication skills of park rangers to define what created the most successful interactions with the public. In his 1957 book, *Interpreting Our Heritage*, Tilden characterized interpretation as "an educational process" that adhered to six specific principles:

1. Relate what is being displayed or described to something within the personality or experience of the visitor.

2. Information, as such, is not interpretation. Interpretation is revelation based upon information. But they are entirely different things. However, all interpretation includes information.

3. Interpretation is an art, which combines many arts, whether the materials presented are scientific, historical, or architectural. Any art is in some degree teachable.

4. The chief aim of interpretation is not instruction, but provocation.

5. Interpretation should aim to present a whole rather than a part, and should address itself to the whole man rather than any phase.

6. Interpretation addressed to children should not be a dilution of the presentation to adults, but should follow a fundamentally different approach.

Essentially, Tilden's principles suggest that interpretation is a specialized form of persuasive communication that must be responsive to specific audiences. Tilden's focus was primarily on personal interpretation, but the principles he identified can also be applied to nonpersonal media.

Tilden wasn't the first to suggest that interpretation is a specialized form of communication with specific aims. Enos Mills, a prolific nature writer and guide who started the first nature guiding school near Rocky Mountain National Park near

■ Freeman Tilden is considered by many to be the father of interpretation.

Estes Park, Colorado, noted that the aim of interpretation is to illuminate big ideas. His work preceded Tilden's but did not have the benefit of promotion by the National Park Service. Still, his *Adventures of a Nature Guide* contains many of the concepts that were later articulated by Tilden's books on the subject.

Forty years after Tilden published *Interpreting Our Heritage*, Ted Cable and Larry Beck updated his principles and added nine more when they wrote *Interpretation for the 21st Century* to address changes brought about by new technology and management techniques. Of specific interest when discussing nonpersonal interpretation, Cable and Beck suggested that:

- High technology must be used with foresight and care.

- Interpreters must concern themselves with the quantity and quality of information presented.

- Interpretive writing should address what readers would like to know, with the authority of wisdom and the humility and care that comes with it.

Definition of Design

As discussed in Lisa Brochu's book *Interpretive Planning*, the term "design" can be used as either a verb or a noun. It is both the act of determining materials, sizes, colors, dimensions, and layout of an interpretive product, and the documented representation or result of that action. In the context of interpretation, design gives form to a planned product, whether that product is an exhibit, a publication, a website, a sign, or some other type of nonpersonal media.

Design is a specialty within the interpretive profession, like planning or program delivery. A well-trained graphic designer has a specific skill set that allows him or her to arrange the elements of design (color, type style, texture, etc.) using principles of repetition, gradation, contrast, proportion, and harmony to create products that communicate a specific message through visual composition. An exhibit designer also has an understanding of industrial or mechanical design with the ability to add three-dimensional elements to the mix. A designer may or may not be an illustrator or artist in the traditional sense, but he or she must have a sense of artistry to develop a product that achieves its stated purpose. (We'll talk more about these specific skill sets in Chapter 4, "Elements of Design.")

Convergence of Interpretation and Design

In a field where many interpretive sites cannot afford on-staff designers or even the fees of occasional freelance designers, the job of producing nonpersonal interpretive media frequently falls to an interpreter with little or no design training. While frontline interpreters usually go through a thorough and systematic process to develop thematic first-person programs, the decision-making processes reflected in many nonpersonal interpretive pieces often get left to computer defaults or what can be produced by hand, sometimes resulting in amateurish, unprofessional products that reflect poorly on the agency or organization.

Since a visitor may have more exposure to nonpersonal media than to an interpreter, the quality of interpretive products must be exceptional to ensure that the desired message is being delivered. In fact, websites and promotional brochures can be even more important than the interpretive programming, as they are often the first contact the public has with a site and serve as the decision point for visitors to determine whether they want to visit the site or participate in a program.

Every time a decision is made in the process of creating nonpersonal interpretive media—from typefaces and colors to the type of media that best suits a project's purposes—this question must be answered: How does this decision support the overall message?

Effectiveness of Nonpersonal Media

The National Park Service (NPS) suggests that in national parks, 62 percent of visitors have contact with nonpersonal media, while only 22 percent have contact with a live interpreter. There is no question that personal interpretation is usually the more effective means of communication, since the interpreter can adapt to individual backgrounds, knowledge levels, and interests of his or her audience, but the NPS statistics (which appear to be similar to those of other interpretive venues) indicate that the burden on nonpersonal media to communicate effectively is substantial.

Many studies have been done to test the effectiveness of design and text on "stop and stay" power. In other words, does the look or feel of the exhibit, sign, publication, or website encourage longer periods of engagement? The assumption behind many of these studies is that if people are more engaged with the medium and are therefore paying more attention to it by staying longer, they are more likely to understand the information being presented and therefore have a greater chance of connecting emotionally and intellectually with the resource. Certainly, if a visitor spends fewer than 10 seconds at a sign (which many studies indicate is the norm), there is little hope that they are seeing or reading more than the title and perhaps getting a vague impression of any images that appear on the sign. At the Peabody Natural History Museum at Yale University, studies indicate that visitors read only about 10 percent of exhibits. Do these studies mean that signs and exhibits and other nonpersonal media are ineffective? Probably not. However, they do mean that planners must work harder to understand what they are trying to achieve with these media selections and designers need to be aware of the challenge in getting visitors to stop, read, look at, interact with, and think about what the media are trying to communicate.

Fewer studies exist on whether the messages delivered through nonpersonal media make any lasting impression on the visitor, which is the real test of effectiveness. However, Sam Ham, author of *Environmental Interpretation*, makes a strong case that people remember themes, not facts. Armed with this knowledge, the planner and designer who work together to create media that communicate a strong theme may be more successful in the long term than those who simply figure out how to display facts and artifacts attractively.

■ Opposite page: An exhibit at the Monterey Bay Aquarium delivers a strong thematic message in its title, supported by graphics, text, and interactive elements.

Ocean wildlife pays a high price for the seafood we eat

SEAFOOD WATCH
a guide for consumers

When it comes to buying seafood, it helps to be choosy

If you like eating seafood, you can keep enjoying it and still protect ocean wildlife. But some seafood is better than others: "good" seafood comes from plentiful populations and well-managed fisheries. "Bad" seafood comes from depleted stocks and harmful fishing practices. Use our *Seafood Watch* card to choose your seafood wisely.

It's easy to buy the right seafood
The aquarium's *Seafood Watch* card helps you decide which kinds of seafood to buy, and which kinds to avoid.

Can fish farms help ocean wildlife?
Farming seafood isn't the answer to saving ocean wildlife. It still takes tons of wild fish— ground into fishmeal—to feed farmed fish.

Please take just one. If you need more, please go to our Information Desk.

How does seafood threaten tunas, turtles and sharks?
Pull the handles to find out.

Interpretive Planning

Interpretive planning is the decision-making process that blends management needs and resource considerations with visitor desire and ability to pay to determine the most effective way to communicate the message to targeted markets, according to Lisa Brochu in *Interpretive Planning*. Ideally, an interpretive plan will be developed for an interpretive site (museum, aquarium, park, etc.) that includes the mix of interpretive products and services that will be used to deliver the messages at that site (programs, exhibits, publications, signs, etc.). This plan is different from a site publication plan or design guidelines document (discussed in Chapter 6, which gives more specific direction on design decisions related to specific types of media). The interpretive plan should also outline design considerations so that the designer can proceed with development of specified products as funding and time allow. If such a plan does not exist, each product should still be planned before design proceeds so that it has the best possible chance of success. The

Planning the Message

remainder of this chapter focuses on the elements that should be considered in planning a product.

Understanding the Audience

Each interpretive product (exhibit, publication, sign, website, or other media) can be targeted to a specific audience. When asked what the intended audience is for a piece, "general public" seems like the easy answer, but the problems caused by this vague description are almost insurmountable in the design process. A piece with a focused message and clearly defined audience, on the other hand, is well on its way to being successful before the first sketch is drawn.

Knowing your audience is the best way to make the piece relevant and create emotional connections. Design features that might appeal to young audiences, such as cartoon characters or especially large and colorful type for early readers, would not necessarily be appropriate for an audience composed primarily of researchers.

When selecting a target market, consider who comes to the site and for whom the message is intended. Not every message is appropriate for every audience. Developing a matrix of audience characteristics and interests may help in determining appropriate messages. Once the audience is clearly identified, another column on the matrix may suggest design characteristics that may appeal to that particular audience and can help spur creativity in the further development of the product.

You can evaluate your audience through surveys, membership information (if yours is a member organization), or simply by careful analysis of who walks through your site's doors. If a specific program is geared toward a specific demographic or interest area (such as middle-aged bird lovers or Civil War enthusiasts), let your design decisions reflect that specificity. If your audience is defined by the function of your project, that also becomes a major influence in your decisions. For instance,

■ An audience/ design matrix helps you develop messages and design choices.

Audience Segment	Characteristics	Interests/ Message	Design Implication
Children Under 12	Early readers; short attention span; attracted to bright colors; strong sense of family	Animals/leave baby birds on the ground	Simple type faces; cartoon features; primary colors
Teens	Not much for reading; some sense of social responsibility developing	Animals/you can volunteer to be a junior keeper	Graphic novel approach; contrasting colors

a brochure placed in a hotel lobby brochure rack will help you identify tourists as your audience, while a direct mail piece lets you know that local residents are your audience. Thinking about how to make these pieces relevant to their specific targets can be challenging, but will yield better results than a general approach that hopes to capture everyone's interest.

When you have identified who is included in your target audience, try to view your project from their point of view instead of your own. What about your site is of most interest to them? What is of least interest? What about your site might surprise a tourist from the other side of the country? What might surprise a local? What would entice the parent of a 10-year-old to bring her child to a program? What is of interest to senior citizens at your site? The more specific you can be with the answers to these questions, the further along you are in the process, even before you begin thinking about layout and design.

Establishing a Purpose

The definition of interpretation establishes that interpretation is mission based, helping to support the purpose of the agency or organization. A designer must therefore understand the mission of the organization to ensure that the visual style and physical attributes of interpretive media convey an appropriate message. For example, if an organization's mission relates to environmental stewardship, using materials that cannot be recycled or reused would send a contradictory, albeit unintentional message. The mission statement can usually be found on an agency's website, in a promotional brochure, or embedded within a master plan or interpretive plan.

Within the parameters of the mission statement and stated goals of the organization, each interpretive product should have a purpose, which can be expressed as a specific, measurable objective with a direct relationship to the mission or goals of the organization. If an interpretive plan that identifies interpretive products to be created has been completed, this purpose will likely be stated in that plan. However, if such a plan does not exist, or if the proposed product is something that is being added to the interpretive mix after the completion of the plan, it becomes imperative that a purpose be identified to guide the design of the product. If a specific purpose cannot be established, then further development of the product may not be in the best interest of the agency or organization.

The objective or purpose of the product should express the desired outcome. Examples include "After viewing the exhibit, 70 percent of visitors will take home a seafood watch pocket guide"

■ Understanding the audience affects design decisions, as with this interactive exhibit for children at the Monterey Bay Aquarium.

and "Enrollment in Saturday family programs will increase by 25 percent after distribution of the brochure." Objectives may reflect increases in sales, volunteerism, participation in programs, or other positive behaviors. They may also suggest decreases in negative behaviors ("Incidents of vandalism to petroglyphs will decline by 80 percent").

On occasion, a cognitive objective may be most appropriate for a specific product, particularly if the product is designed for a student audience that can be tested in a formal education setting after a site visit. For example: "Eighty percent of students will correctly identify three species of wildlife in the park." Such objectives will be even more powerful if they are aligned with local school standards. Although cognitive objectives work well for school groups who may be required to learn something (or attempt to, anyway) during their visit, most casual or family visitors to interpretive sites are not interested in achieving cognitive objectives and would be difficult to test. Remember that these individuals have come to your site by choice and can easily leave if they are bored or feel intimidated by a didactic approach. What's worse, they are likely to tell others to avoid your site in the future if they did not enjoy the experience. For these target audiences, behavioral objectives that describe observable results will be the better measure of success.

Once the purpose of your communication has been determined, design elements can be selected that will enhance the likelihood of achieving the specific objective. For example, if the message is authoritative, a typeface that reinforces the authority of the message can be selected (see Chapter 4 for a more thorough discussion of the use of typography).

Resource Implications

Every interpretive site has resources to interpret. In a museum setting, the resource may be the collection and the stories associated with the artifacts on display. At a national park, the resources may be the stories that play out over a dramatic landscape or in a historic building. A nature center may focus on local ecosystems as its resource base. Regardless of the resource, the interpretive planning process should reveal the significance of what is to be interpreted.

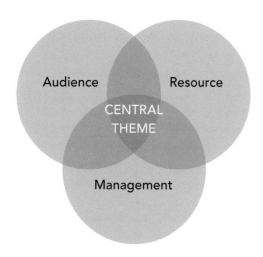

■ The central theme should be a reflection of audience interest, resource considerations, and management needs.

Developing a Thematic Story

Once you understand the relationships between the triad of audience, resource, and management (purpose), you can begin to craft the thematic messages you hope to communicate through nonpersonal media. Most interpretive sites will develop a central theme that serves as the umbrella for all communications. In other words, each exhibit, brochure, sign, or other medium will somehow relate to the bigger picture of the central theme so that the visitor comes away with an awareness of the site's significance. That theme is usually identified in the interpretive plan, so that when a new exhibit or publication is planned, the direct link to the theme can be easily established. If that link cannot be established, perhaps your site is not the best place to be telling the story. For example, the Grand Canyon may not be the best place to tell the story of the effect of global climate change on polar bears, but it is a wonderful place to help people understand the importance and power of water through geologic time. Ideally, the central theme combines what the audience is interested in, the significance of the resource (which may not be the same thing as what the audience is interested in), and what management wants or needs to communicate about that resource to the audience.

The interpretive plan may then divide the theme into supporting subthemes (see the sidebar on page 12), which are supported by individual storylines. This framework is an organizing tool that allows you to focus your efforts on appropriate communications instead of veering into "polar bear" territory, or stories that would be better told elsewhere. Those storylines will form the basis for individual interpretive pieces, though more than one storyline may appear on a single exhibit or brochure.

Once you have your storylines identified, you can begin to match them to specific target audiences with specific media. This approach provides guidance for whether you need a brochure, a book, an exhibit, a sign, an audio tour, or some other type of media to communicate your message effectively.

	Subtheme A	Subtheme B	Subtheme C
Birders	Exhibit on birdsongs at visitor center		Trail sign 1
Hikers		Trail sign 2	
Boaters			Wayside exhibit at boat dock
Picnickers	Signs at pavilion		
Campers		Wayside exhibit at amphitheater	Trail sign 3

■ A media/ message matrix helps match the best format for communicating specific themes to target audiences.

Themes, Subthemes, and Storylines

The Boulder County (Colorado) Parks and Open Space Department developed exhibits at the Agricultural Heritage Center to remind visitors of their relationship to the land through interpretation of the county's agricultural past, present, and future. A central theme was developed for the site to tie together the variety of venues where interpretive media were used. The thematic framework for development of the exhibits looked like this:

Central Theme of Site
Agriculture sowed the seeds for a century of change in Boulder County.

Theme of Stroh/Dickens Barn Exhibits
The Stroh/Dickens barn holds 100 years of history in its massive framework.

Subtheme 1)
A succession of families has used this barn.

Storyline A: The Dickens family built the barn around 1900 and used it for only about six years.

Storyline B: The Hansen/Johnson family leased the barn from the Dickens family from 1906 until 1928.

Storyline C: The Stroh family bought the farm (and barn) from the Dickens family in 1928.

Storyline D: Parks and Open Space bought the barn and moved it to this site in 1998 for use by families as an enjoyable educational experience.

Subtheme 2)
Farming is often a challenge.

Storyline A: By the time the barn was built, the Rocky Mountain locust invasion was just a memory.

Storyline B: The 1900 flood, 1913 blizzard, and dust bowl era of the 1920s and 1930s typified some of the environmental challenges faced by farmers.

Storyline C: The sugar beet and other vegetable industries were subject to blights.

Storyline D: Seasons dictate the farm's daily life.

Subtheme 3)
Farming has changed dramatically in the last 100 years.

Storyline A: Pesticides have both negative and positive effects depending on the methods used.

Storyline B: Dryland farming methods allowed Boulder County farms to survive.

Storyline C: Modern irrigation methods are more efficient than historical methods.

Storyline D: The power that drives the farm has evolved from horses to steam engine to gas engine.

Storyline E: Many cultures have influenced farming in Boulder County.

Storyline F: Boulder County's relationship to agriculture and open space looks to the past and to the future.

BOULDER COUNTY PARKS AND OPEN SPACE / CONDIT EXHIBITS

■ Themes, subthemes, and storylines help create a coherent, memorable message. The above exhibit, "Horsepower on the Hoof," addresses Storyline D under Subtheme 3, and is complemented by a facing exhibit titled "Horsepower Under the Hood."

Choosing a Medium

The phrase "Form follows function" dates back to 19th-century American sculptor Horatio Greenough, and its wisdom still rings true today. The best way to choose what type of interpretive media suits your site's needs is to think about how the information will be used. It's easy to think, simply, "We need a brochure," and set to work on laying out a tri-fold brochure because that's what is familiar. But contemplating the nature of the information you wish to disseminate may change what type of media you want to use.

Is the information intended to help visitors plan a visit? A website offers the most bang for the buck, as it is accessible from around the world and can be frequently updated. Websites can be your site's first contact with a potential visitor, and they are frequently more informational than interpretive. But the best websites reference the important themes of the sites they represent. Mailed promotional materials help entice potential visitors if the targeted audience is within a finite community. These are best used to promote specific events like a night hike at a nature center or a reenactment at a historical site. Is the content of your piece mostly used on-site? Maps and guides should be portable, preferably so that they fit in a pocket—otherwise they risk getting left behind and their message is lost. They should be durable enough to be folded and refolded during the visit, but easy to recycle or file away for another visit. If the information is not subject to frequent change, wayside exhibits or kiosks may offer more permanent solutions.

For more detailed information about the finer points of individual types of media, see Chapter 6.

Interpretive Writing

No matter what type of media you develop, interpretive writing will be part of it. Interpretive writing is different than writing for a newspaper or research journal. What are the differences between technical writing, journalism, creative writing, and interpretive writing? Interpretive writing may contain elements of the other three styles, but it is specifically considered interpretive writing when it adheres to the interpretive principles previously stated. Technical writing seeks to provide information (think instructions for installing a dishwasher). Journalism tells a story, imparting information in a more enjoyable way (think newspaper story about a local hero), but does not necessarily move beyond the story to provoke further thought or action or provide any specific message. It covers the who, what, where, why, and when, but may not go much further. Creative writing uses language to paint verbal pictures. It is engaging and descriptive (think about a favorite poem), but may not meet the test of being provocative and thematic.

Interpretive writing reveals information in an enjoyable, provocative, audience-specific, thematic style, using examples that help make the text more relevant to the reader. Interpretive writers are those who are able to communicate through the written word using interpretive principles. It seems simple enough, but very often, writing tasks are given to someone on staff who may not be familiar with interpretive principles. There seems to be some feeling that because someone can craft a coherent sentence, that's all that matters. But think about what you're trying to communicate. How important is it to get that message across and have it stick? If you're the biologist, you may think the biological facts are incredibly

Can you See the Swamp?

This land was once very different.
If you could travel back through time—160 million years ago to this same spot—you'd be up to your knees in a swampy mud flat. Today, however, all that remains of that prehistoric swamp are the red hills across the canyon—made of petrified mud with occasional fossil clues to the primeval past.

"Ancient Arizona" can carry you back in time. This exhibit will give you:
• several views into southern Arizona's deep past
• the story of Sonorasaurus—a major dinosaur discovery
• an introduction to paleontology
• a chance to excavate your own "fossil"

■ This sign from the Arizona-Sonora Desert Museum in Tucson is a good example of keeping a low word count and avoiding jargon.

important—after all, who wouldn't be fascinated by the average height, weight, and feeding habits of a 13-lined ground squirrel? But the reality is, people don't tend to retain these facts and they aren't always germane to the real message about the importance of the ground squirrel to the ecosystem.

Some "ologists" are excellent interpretive writers, but more often than not, they tend to dwell on the facts that they find most interesting and forget that they are not talking to other "ologists." The audience usually doesn't have a scientific background or much more than a passing interest in the subject matter. Let's face it, if you are not a paleontologist, the names of various time periods (Jurassic,

Cretaceous, Devonian) are not gripping material. What's more, that's okay. It probably isn't going to accomplish anything to insist that your visitors attempt to learn technical information that doesn't have any relevance to their lives. On the other hand, if you're trying to get them to understand why fossil fuels are a nonrenewable resource, you might want to talk about how many lifetimes it took to create the gas they put in the car that morning and get them to think about what happens when there is no more oil to convert into gas. That puts dinosaurs in perspective in a way that epoch names do not.

Generally, it's a good idea to ask your staff resource specialists to draft text that might be used for a sign, publication, exhibit, or audio program. That draft should then be handed to an interpretive writer to massage it into something that will be meaningful to visitors. If you don't feel confident with your interpretive writing skills, it's time to contract out for a final edit and polish. You can find interpretive writers in the National Association for Interpretation's *Interpreter's Green Pages.* Or you can ask other sites with great writing who did the work for them. If you want to tackle the writing or editing job yourself, the following tips may help you refine your work. Alan Leftridge's book *Interpretive Writing* is also recommended for additional information about the subject.

Cut the word count.

Brevity matters for two reasons. First, your visitor's attention span may be significantly shorter than you think it should be. Some studies indicate that the average visitor spends fewer than 10 seconds in front of a sign unless that sign is completely captivating. It's hard to read and comprehend more than 50 words in 10 seconds, much less have time to reflect on what's been read in any thoughtful way. A good rule of thumb is no more than 150 to 200 words on any one sign, exhibit, or brochure panel, ideally broken up into paragraphs of 50 or fewer words each. If the concept you're trying to convey requires more words, think about writing a booklet or longer publication that can explore the idea in more detail for those who have the interest.

The second reason to keep your word count low is in deference to the designer. Fewer words mean more space to work with "white space" or images, both of which will add impact by emphasizing your words. Writers sometimes succumb to the temptation to describe an image in detail. Let the image do the work and choose your words carefully so that the text block or caption amplifies the image and vice versa, instead of being repetitive.

The easiest ways to cut your word count include avoiding adverbs and redundant adjectives, removing unnecessary usage of "the," selecting action verbs and active voice instead of passive sentences that rely on variations of the verb "to be," and avoiding run-on sentences. Write a draft, edit for fewer words, then do it again. And again. And maybe a fourth time. Editing to make your point in the fewest words possible is an art form, but practice will help you get better. You may want to practice by taking a few samples of writing from around your site and attempting to rewrite them before you have to face the creation of an entirely new project.

Avoid jargon.

Technical language belongs in technical writing, not interpretive writing. Do not assume that everyone knows what "riparian" means just because you use the term on a daily basis. If you decide to use a term that is not usually found in mainstream conversation, be sure to define it in terms your audience will understand. And in spite of today's trend toward abbreviated text messaging, using acronyms that are not commonly known will confuse your audience. Leave the abbreviations on your cell phone, not in your interpretive text. On the other hand, explaining how some terms have come into common usage can sometimes be an interesting sidebar (for instance, SCUBA is a commonly used term that actually stands for Self-Contained Underwater Breathing Apparatus).

Keep it simple.

Knowing the audience should influence the readability of your work. Before the advent of word processing programs, readability could be checked manually by using a mathematical formula such as the Fog Index, which measures readability by assessing the number of "hard" words and the complexity of sentences. The result of the computations yields a grade level that indicates the approximate readability of the work. Most computer software can check readability for you with the touch of a button. In Microsoft Word,™ for example, a user can check "show readability statistics" under the spelling and grammar preferences and the program will automatically calculate the readability of a selection. For most interpretive pieces designed for family audiences, strive for an eighth-grade level that will be understood by 75 percent of more of your audience (the Flesch scale used in Microsoft Word will provide that information). The eighth-grade reading level is the typical standard for newspapers and magazines such as *Reader's Digest* that appeal to mass audiences. For specific target audiences, adjust the readability accordingly (down for a children's exhibit, up for a Ph.D. audience).

Watch your language.
If you provide multilingual text on any print material (including signs, exhibits, or publications), be aware that you will likely use one and a half times the space for the second language. This has profound implications for text and layout of text or image elements, decreasing significantly the amount of space for both. If you would normally allow 150 words for an all-English sign, for example, you are now limited to 50 words in English because your second language version will take the remaining space.

Follow rules of grammar.
Good interpretive writing is also good writing, period. Pay attention to sentence structure, subject-verb agreement, changes in tense, and all other generally accepted rules of grammar.

Do some testing with potential audience members to determine whether your message is clear.
Focus groups or complete strangers work well for this. Don't test with colleagues—their knowledge level and bias will be similar to yours and so will not give you a true reading on how your text will be received.

■ Expect a second language to take more space than English, as with this sign in Brecon Beacon National Park in Wales.

Don't date yourself.

We're not talking about making emotional attachments, but rather the use of trendy catchphrases that will quickly become passé. Some expressions are timeless and universal, while others make no sense to those born a decade earlier or later than you. Use actual years or dates instead of phrases like "10 years ago" or "10 years from now." Think about the accuracy of those phrases if your words will still be visible to the public 20 years after the sign is written. Your words must provide a frame of reference that will remain current in case your organization's budget doesn't lend itself to makeovers every few years. If, on the other hand, you're writing a temporary piece that will only be in use for three months to a year, use the current pop culture as appropriate to tap into market interest.

Copyediting

When you think you have a final draft of your written materials, send it for one last edit by a trained copyeditor. This person will check for grammatical errors, punctuation, appropriate use of citations, and anything else that might trip up a reader. He or she will usually flag phrases that may be confusing and ask if you really meant to say, "Some fish swim away after being eaten by piranhas." It doesn't hurt to have a copyeditor check the text before turning it over to the designer and then again after the design process to ensure that lines of text or punctuation haven't inadvertently been dropped out of a text block. Some designers take the initiative to edit text to make it fit the space; if that occurs and the designer doesn't have any background with your material, he or she may change your meaning without realizing it. A good copyeditor familiar with your site's resources will keep everyone on track and ensure that your product makes sense.

■ Even on small projects, a good copyeditor helps. A proofreader would have prevented this error on six metal signs in Richmond, Virginia.

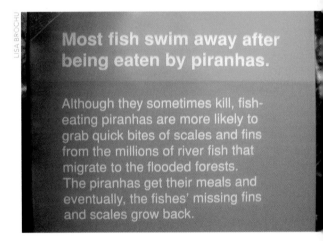

■ A copyeditor will help you steer clear of confusing phrases.

■ Opposite page:
Hand-crafted
glass outside
the Tacoma
Glass Museum
in Tacoma,
Washington.

LISA BROCHU

The Creative Design Process

The term creative process evokes images of sandal-wearing slackers picking flowers in the meadow, daydreaming about what a project might look like without actually doing anything. Creativity flows in individuals in different ways. In truth, the process can be systematic and orderly. Obstacles like production schedules and conflicting feedback can be frustrating, but if you have been assigned the task of creating a product, then final decisions rest with you. It is your responsibility to take control of the process and make it happen rather than sitting back and hoping it happens.

Precedents

If you are creating a website, surf the Web to see what works and what doesn't. If you are creating a newsletter, find other newsletters and look at them with a critical eye. Look for elements that you like and elements that you would like to avoid. Look beyond your own demographic and branch into other areas. If you are cre-

The Design Process

ating a piece for a small nature center, look at other nature centers, but also look at historical sites, aquaria, restaurants, multinational conglomerate financial institutions, local yard sales, and so on. Inspiration is everywhere. As you mesh borrowed elements with your own, your own voice (or, more appropriately, the voice of the institution that is paying you) will shine through.

More frequently than not, you will not directly copy (or "reappropriate," if that helps alleviate the guilt) elements from the pieces that catch your eye. Rather, this phase of the process will stimulate ideas and the end result will be completely different from the pieces that inspired you. Sometimes, though, you will see a specific color palette, layout, or typographic treatment that speaks to you. It's okay to use these elements, as long as they are not trademarked and they support the message of your piece.

Inspiration in the Environment

Outside lies utterly ordinary space open to any casual explorer willing to find the extraordinary. Outside lies unprogrammed awareness that at times becomes directed serendipity. Outside lies magic.

—John Stilgoe, *Outside Lies Magic*

Creative inspiration can strike at the strangest moments—falling asleep at night, walking through the grocery store, or strolling down the street. Your mind is constantly at work, and the solution to a design problem can pop into your head like the name of a movie actor or song you tried to think of for 20 minutes and then gave up on. However, this doesn't mean you should dawdle and wait for answers to sneak up behind you and bite you on the back side. Go out into the environment and study it. Look at written words on everything from handwritten yard sale signs to the neon lights of chain restaurants. Look at color combinations that you find in the built or natural environment. Look up, look down, squint, and intentionally unfocus your eyes. You might not find the exact answers you're looking for just outside your front door, but the process gets the creative juices flowing.

And most importantly, carry a digital camera or a sketch pad. If you take enough notice to document something that catches your eye, it is worth revisiting later to study in further detail.

■ Who knows what might catch your eye when you least expect it? Carry a camera or a sketch pad to take advantage of unexpected inspiration.

Right Brain and Left Brain

Roger W. Sperry received the Nobel Prize in Physiology or Medicine in 1981 "for his discoveries concerning the functional specialization of the cerebral hemispheres." It was Sperry who introduced us to the theory that the left side of the brain wears a bow tie and carries a calculator (dealing with logical, analytical, rational thinking) and that the right side of the brain wears sandals and picks flowers in the meadow (dealing with intuitive, subjective, holistic thinking).

While some people lean toward either the bow tie or sandal camp, it's important to recognize that the creative process relies on both sides of the brain. Sperry's research tells us that the sandal-wearers on the right have more aptitude for aesthetics and looking at the whole, but while it is important that your piece be attractive, graphic design is about more than just aesthetics. It's about organizing and conveying information in a systematic way. The bow ties on the left bring logic and analysis to the table, which is every bit as important, if not more so. The left side of the brain explains and justifies the artistic decisions that the right side makes. And if an artistic or aesthetic decision cannot be explained through logic or rationale—if it does not stand up to analysis—then it is probably not the correct decision.

Brainstorming

Brainstorming—generating and listing ideas without any judgment of whether they are good or bad—leads to free thinking. If you automatically dismiss ideas because you think they are too expensive, will never be approved, or are over the top, you miss the opportunity to create an idea that works. Brainstorming can be a group process, where participants generate ideas through conversation with one person recording those ideas. The group dynamic is extremely important, as the process will not work if participants feel inhibited about speaking freely. Brainstorming can also be a solo act, where one individual focuses on the topic at hand and comes up with a list of ideas or related thoughts.

Brainstorming often works best if you put yourself in an unfamiliar environment. If you work in an office all day, behind a desk, staring at a computer, it may be hard to break your normal thought process. Find a location where you will not be distracted by your normal day-to-day operations. Group brainstorming sessions can occur anywhere from a formal staff retreat to a cup of coffee with a select few participants. Individual sessions can happen wherever and whenever—on a bike ride, during a commute, even standing in line at the bank.

■ Inspiration in the environment: These different shades of green at Olympic National Park in Washington could inspire an interesting color palette for a printed piece.

■ A production schedule begins with knowing the date your printer or manufacturer needs digital files from the designer to assure timely delivery of the finished product:

August 20: Materials (photos, text, advertisements, etc.) due to designer.

September 10: First draft from designer circulated for review.

September 17: Comments from reviewers due.

September 24: Final draft from designer circulated for review.

September 25–30: Reviewers or client have the opportunity to suggest minor changes.

September 30: Reviewers or client approve final draft.

October 1: Designer delivers files to printer or manufacturer.

October 15: Printer or manufacturer delivers product.

Schedule

Nothing spurs the procrastinating mind like a looming deadline. This is why a production schedule—even if the deadlines are self-imposed—is an important tool in the creative process. Sometimes the dates on a schedule are real. The November issue of a newsletter has to go to press in early to mid-October (depending on printing and mailing schedules) to be delivered to recipients in a timely fashion. Sometimes deadlines are arbitrary. A new logo will be unveiled at some unspecified time in the next year, but you assign a specific date to have the first batch of sketches prepared for review. As with any element of the creative process, this works better with some than with others. The late humorist and author Douglas Adams once said, "I love deadlines. I like the whooshing sound they make as they fly by."

The best way to create a production schedule is by working backwards. Suppose you're creating program guides for an event that takes place at your site on October 15. Work with your printer to establish the date by which they need electronic files to assure timely delivery (October 1, for the purposes of this example). Then, using this date, give yourself enough time to lay out a first draft (by September 10), allow for review and comments (by September 17), implement changes (by September 24), and circulate a final draft and receive approval before sending files to your printer. Given these dates, you know that you need to have information ready or receive materials from those who are preparing them by the end of August to meet the demands of your schedule. (Of course, the example above is just that, an example. Be sure to give yourself all the time you need and build some slack into your own schedule.) Be firm with people who are providing materials or feedback to be sure they meet your schedule. They may not be thinking about an event that takes place in mid-October during August, but it's your job to make sure those program guides are there.

Feedback

It's important to realize and to accept that you cannot please everybody all the time, especially when it comes to the visual representation of a resource or organization that inspires deep emotional connections, as so many interpretive sites do. Still, soliciting and synthesizing feedback is a crucial part of the creative process. As a designer, your job is to convey the voice and message of others. Be able to explain and defend your decisions, but be willing to listen to those who don't believe you've achieved what you set out to achieve.

It's not necessary to seek approval on a project from every

single person involved with that project, and you will seem needy and uncertain of your talents if you ask for input on every design decision you make. But if you are designing something relatively permanent that represents an organization—a website, a logo, or a template for a newsletter or magazine, for instance—take your product to a focus group before you unleash it on the audience at large. A focus group can be as small as 10 to 20 individuals you trust to be forthright and honest with you or as large as 500 people selected at random.

Look for consistent results from your focus group and be willing to dismiss the rambling diatribe that comes from that one person who clearly has an agenda or whose input is wildly different from all the others. As the designer, it is your responsibility to evaluate which criticisms are valid and which are not. Frequently, feedback will validate concerns you had about a project in the first place. Be aware that focus groups will tend to be conservative. If you are pushing the envelope or presenting something out of your audience's comfort zone, be ready for negative input. But if you are confident in your design, able to defend it, and willing to take the heat, go for it.

You can also solicit feedback from individuals outside your organization. Ask friends, family, or strangers to react to a certain typeface or color palette. Ask specific questions like "What one word or phrase would you use to describe the personality of this typeface?" or "What do these colors make you think of?" to test the validity of your decisions.

Collaboration

So much of successful design lies in collaboration. While your responsibility as the designer is to organize and synthesize text and image, those materials frequently come from other people. You will work with writers, photographers, editors, and other interested parties. As the designer, you are responsible for directing those individuals to suit the needs of the project.

Of course, the danger of collaboration is that too many disparate voices can lead to muddied, flimsy communication. Be sure to establish a strong message from the beginning and communicate it clearly to anyone who contributes to the project. The best way to do this is through a written theme statement (something like "Interpretation of sacred sites promotes understanding between cultures.") that you can provide to all contributors. (See Chapter 2 for more on crafting a message.) This not only helps those you work with understand the project, but it is a great way to clarify your intent to yourself as you get started. Make sure everyone is informed of and agrees upon other important information such as target audience, deadlines, and any other specific needs that you have for your project. (See Chapter 7 for more on the collaborative process.)

■ Opposite page:
Hand-painted sign
on Culebra Island,
Puerto Rico.

Color

Think of your favorite vacation spot. What colors do you associate with it? More importantly, why do you associate those colors with that place? The most likely reason to associate a color with a place is that it relates to a natural feature found there. Organizations that deal with nature almost invariably use a shade of green. Most aquaria use blue as a part of their identities, lest the visitor forget there's water in the building.

The hand-painted "Leatherback Turtle Nesting Area" sign above was found on Culebra Island off the coast of Puerto Rico. The blue-green background clearly relates to the color of the Caribbean water just yards away. The magenta/purple of the lettering was most likely an intuitive decision—it interacts with the blue-green to create a pleasing tropical palette that is consistent with the emotion one feels basking in the peace of this Caribbean scene. The message of this sign is far stronger because of the way it uses color to reinforce a connection with the place. There's so much to like about this piece of communication; the fact that it's hand painted,

Elements of Design

rather than making it look unprofessional, communicates to the visitor that someone cared enough about these turtles to create this and many other signs on the same beach one at a time. A synthetic, black-and-white, type-set sign would not have had the same effect.

Color can also represent a cultural or historical resource or organization. Go to Albuquerque and you will find turquoise not just in the jewelry at the public market, but in practically every piece of literature that relates to the area. Historic sites rely on sepia tones to convey a sense of antiquity, relating to the color of photographs from a certain era. Even if a site is dealing with a time period other than the early days of photography, the warm brown of a sepia tone alerts the viewer that he or she is looking at material from days gone by.

Other reasons to select a color are less obvious, but every bit as valid. The color palette many associate with Latin America features bright yellows and reds, vivid warm colors that evoke the architecture of the area and convey a sense of vitality and love of life. Red can also convey danger or alarm. Blues and greens have a calming effect. There are countless reasons a color can be meaningful to your organization, site, or resource. What is most important in terms of selecting a color is that you have a reason for it and can defend that reason if pressed.

Color Schemes

Once you have decided on a color or series of colors appropriate to your resource, an understanding of the color wheel, the brain-child of Sir Isaac Newton in 1666, will guide you in establishing a color scheme. While color palettes can derive from a number of sources (colors found in nature, colors associated with certain emotions, etc.), the color wheel is an invaluable resource that will help you understand how colors work together to achieve certain effects. High-frequency versus low-frequency color schemes and complementary and analogous color pairings can greatly affect the communication you create.

The color wheel in its most basic form is made up of the three primary colors: red, yellow, and blue. These pigments are the only three that cannot be created by a combination of other colors. When used as a color scheme, this "primary triad" creates a look that is extremely basic, even childish. In design circles, it is some-times even called the "Fisher Price Triad" because many children's toys feature these colors.

In its next level of complexity, the color wheel introduces secondary colors—orange, purple, and green—created by mixing two adjacent primary colors. (Red and blue make purple; blue and yellow make green; yellow and red make orange.)

■ Primary colors
red, yellow, and blue are the building blocks of all other colors.

■ Secondary colors orange, purple, and green are created by combining two primary colors.

■ Tertiary colors like yellow-orange and blue-green are created by mixing primary and secondary colors that are adjacent to each other on the color wheel.

The Vancouver Aquarium in Vancouver, Canada, takes advantage of a strong complementary color scheme in its jellyfish exhibit.

PAUL CAPUTO

Combining adjacent primary and secondary colors creates tertiary colors, such as yellow-orange, red-orange, red-purple, blue-purple, blue-green, and yellow-green. Tertiary (or "third") colors frequently go by other names (blue-green can be aqua or turquoise, red-purple can be burgundy, yellow-green can be lime, etc.). When the color wheel includes tertiary colors, it contains 12 colors. (The color wheel can be expanded to include a nearly infinite number of hues.)

Basic formulas for color harmony include complementary, analogous, and monochromatic. The most appropriate formula depends on the type of message you wish to convey or mood you strive to create. Complementary colors are those found opposite each other on the color wheel. Complementary pairs include blue and orange, red and green, and yellow and purple. (Color combinations that include pairs of colors opposite each other on the color wheel, like orange and yellow-orange paired with blue and blue-purple, are called "split complements.") These combinations achieve maximum contrast, and therefore create the boldest look. Analogous colors are any two or three adjacent colors on a 12-part color wheel, like yellow, yellow-green, and green. These combinations are low in contrast, creating a subtle, soothing look. A monochromatic color scheme is based on a single hue (or color) from the color wheel, creating contrast and variation through tints (adding white) and shades (adding black). Monochromatic color schemes are often born of necessity with budgets that limit printing jobs to just one color, but they can be quite effective if shades or screens of one color are used to give the illusion of depth of color.

Complementary colors are opposite each other on the color wheel and create high contrast.

Analogous colors are adjacent to each other on the color wheel and create low contrast.

A monochromatic color scheme includes only one color with contrast created by adding black (shades) or white (tints).

Vocabulary of Color

There are many ways to talk about color, but the following terms are common and useful:

Hue: A color. A hue of red is 100 percent red, with no white or black diluting it.

Tint: A hue plus white. The higher the degree of tint, the lighter the color.

Shade: A hue plus black. The higher the degree of shade, the darker the color.

Intensity/Saturation: These two terms refer to the purity of a color (a color at 100 percent intensity or saturation contains no white or black).

■ Warm colors: Yellow, orange, and red advance, or pop out, on compositions.

Warm Colors: Yellow, orange, and red. These colors are associated with warmth because they evoke things like sunlight and fire. Warm colors are generally considered to convey a sense of movement and energy, and to be more personal and intimate than cool colors. In a composition, warm colors advance, or jump out.

■ Cool colors: Green, blue, and purple recede on compositions.

Cool Colors: Green, blue, and purple (although purple can easily become warm if the balance of red and blue tilts toward red, its effect is generally considered to be cool). These colors are associated with cold temperatures because they evoke water and ice. They have a calming effect and create a sense of emotional distance. In a composition, cool colors recede.

Neutral Colors: Gray and brown. These are made by mixing complementary colors.

For information on working with color on the computer, see Chapter 5, "Technical Specifications."

Typography

Typeface vs. Font

The terms typeface and font tend be used interchangeably, especially since the advent of computers, but they technically have different meanings. A typeface is a set of fonts. For instance, Helvetica, Helvetica bold, Helvetica italics, and Helvetica bold italics are four distinct fonts, but they are all part of one typeface.

Selecting Typefaces

It is tempting and all too easy to leave the selection of typefaces to your computer's default selections; however, it is essential that you seize control of this decision. The typefaces you choose are your visual voice. They determine the personality of the finished piece, set the tone for design decisions still to come, and are the first step toward creating legible communication.

Think of some words that describe the voice you want to establish (organic, bold, elegant, etc.) and use this list to guide your selection. Be ready to defend your choice if you're asked what it says about the organization or site you're representing. It's best to know what sort of typeface you're looking for before you even turn on your computer. If you can't find what you're looking for in the pre-established pull-down menus that came with your computer, it's time to start perusing online resources or printed typeface catalogs. Once you have selected a typeface that you think conveys the characteristics you wish to convey, print out one word or even a single letter in that typeface and show it to co-workers, friends, and even strangers in the grocery store (or wherever). Ask for a one-word description of the characteristics of your typeface. You may be surprised at what you find (and if you are, then it's back to the drawing board—literally).

Typefaces can be divided into countless categories. We look here at three basic subsets.

Serifs (like Garamond and Times) are those typefaces made up of varying stroke widths with "feet" at the end of each stroke. The word serif is used to describe the short strokes at the end of longer strokes on letterforms. There's some debate about the origin of the word. One popular but unproven theory is that it comes from the Latin *seraphim*, for "wings." Look closely and you will see how serif typefaces derived from calligraphy and other hand-drawn letterforms. They are typically used as body text in printed materials (as is the case in this book), and help establish a classical, refined look.

Sans serifs (like Helvetica and Arial) are made up of consistent stroke widths and have little or no ornamentation. The term sans-serif derives from the French *sans,* meaning "without." Sans-serif typefaces do not include "wings" or "feet." They create a clean, simple look, but the uniform stroke width makes them less legible as body text. While they are more modern in their look and feel, derived from mathematical formulas and mechanical production methods, sans serifs date back hundreds of years (for example, dates etched into cornerstones of many historic buildings around the world were done so in sans serif), but they did not become widely used until the modernist movement of the 20th century.

The third category of typeface can politely be described as decorative or less politely as gimmicky. These range from faux handwriting like Comic Sans or Chalkboard to a historical blackletter like Old English and everything in between. Tread carefully when you encounter a decorative typeface. It is easy

■ Serif fonts have "feet" or "wings" and are classical or traditional.

■ Sans-serif fonts have consistent stroke widths and are more modern.

■ Decorative fonts are more whimsical and should be used sparingly.

to overwhelm your audience by relying on a typeface that is expressive, but difficult to read. Some typefaces seem chock full of personality, conveying everything you want to say about your site, but as soon as you select it, you may suddenly notice that the same typeface has been used 100 times over by other, very different organizations (if that typeface is a default on your computer, it's probably a default on everyone else's computer). Materials that rely on a gimmicky typeface can look unprofessional.

Your typeface choice should be consistent with the identity you are trying to establish for your organization, but remember that it does not have to say everything about it. A poorly selected typeface will interfere with the identity you intend to create or message you wish to convey. A well-selected typeface will feel almost obvious once you have found it. Unfortunately, your audience will notice and possibly be annoyed by a poorly selected typeface right away, but a well-selected typeface will seem like it just fell into place on the page because it belonged there all along. The best typefaces are those that will help convey messages clearly and establish moods without drawing an excessive amount of attention to themselves.

Basic Rules of Typography

Noted surfer dude and graphic designer David Carson once said, "Never mistake legibility for communication." What he meant was that type does not have to be legible to communicate emotions or messages. Taken another, more practical way, Carson's statement means that the way type is treated on a page has as much ability to convey messages as the words themselves.

Typography is an art, and designers use its subtle tools to communicate through nuance. Legibility should always be a goal of interpretive media, but the level of communication should not end there. Many beginners make the mistake of thinking that their ability to communicate through type ends when they have selected a typeface. Some of the points of discussion below relate to maximizing legibility while others are geared toward emotive or expressive qualities of typesetting.

Do not use too many typefaces. The biggest mistake novice designers make is to clutter their projects with too many typefaces. For most projects, choose two typefaces and stick with them. The best approach is to select one primary typeface, typically a serif, which should be used for body text, and then pick a very different typeface, a sans serif, to provide contrast where it's needed, such as in a title or subtitle.

For instance, the body copy of this book is set in Minion, a serif typeface designed in the classical tradition. Captions, subheads, and other highlighted materials are set in Avenir, a sans serif (whose name means "future" in French).

Okay, maybe one more typeface. The only reason to introduce a third typeface would be if you have a decorative typeface that is closely associated with your site or organization's identity. In this case, a third typeface is acceptable, but only if it is used sparingly and exclusively as display type—one or two words per page at most. Used as display type, a decorative typeface acts almost like an image and does not interfere with the two typefaces you've selected for the bulk of your copy.

You will notice that the word "Design" on the cover of this book and the chapter numbers within are set in a decorative typeface (called "FFF Tusj") that relates conceptually to the notion of sketching or designing. In this case, the third typeface is treated as an image rather than type.

Contrast is key. When using more than one typeface on a page, make sure they create contrast and are not too similar. Never choose two similar-looking typefaces; it will only create confusion.

Avoid widows and orphans whenever possible. A widow is a single word or very short line of text at the end of a paragraph. An orphan is a single syllable of a hyphenated word on a line by itself at the end of a paragraph. A loose rule of thumb is that if you have five or fewer characters making up one line at the end of a paragraph, it's too short. You can make minor changes to letter or word spacing to avoid widows in your composition. A widow looks like this.

And regardless of how many characters are in the line, the last line of a paragraph should never appear at the top of a column. Do whatever it takes to end the paragraph at the bottom of the previous column or extend the paragraph by a line or two.

Always maintain the integrity of type. One of the most offensive side effects of the personal computer is the degradation of typefaces that have been painstakingly crafted over the course of decades. In most recognized typefaces, individual letterforms have been designed by passionate artisans—sometimes hundreds of years ago—dedicated to creating perfectly balanced, legible characters. Don't undo their work by stretching, squishing, squeezing, or otherwise violating these letterforms, even if image-editing and page-layout programs make it easy to do so.

Don't stack type. Words are meant to be read from left to right, not top to bottom. Letters are meant to interact with each other side by side. If you want or need to run type vertically, turn the whole word sideways to maximize legibility. (You should avoid using vertical or angled type on a sign or exhibit, where it may discourage readers from taking the extra time to understand the message.)

Use upper- and lower-case letters. Readers recognize words as shapes rather than as series of individual letters, so words written in all capital letters are less legible than words written in upper and lower case.

WORDS WRITTEN IN ALL CAPS BECOME UNIFORM, BLOCKY RECTANGLES, AND REQUIRE MORE EFFORT TO READ.

Words written with upper- and lower-case letterforms have more distinct shapes and are more recognizable, especially at a distance. If you choose to use all capitals (which you should do sparingly, and only in the instance of display type), loosen the letter spacing.

LIKE THIS

This helps readers distinguish the individual letterforms more quickly and increases legibility.

■ Just because you can doesn't mean you should. Don't stretch or squish letters.

DON'T DO THIS! DO THIS INSTEAD!

■ Letters are meant to interact side by side. Stacking type makes it less legible.

tight
loose

■ Letter spacing on display type, when using upper- and lower-case letters, should be as tight as possible.

■ This type is set at 10 over 14 (with a point size of 10 and the leading set at 14).

■ This type is set at 12 over 18 (with a point size of 12 and the leading set at 18).

Tighter letter spacing for lower-case letters is more legible. When you are dealing with lower-case letters, the tighter you can make your letter spacing while still maintaining some space between the letters, the more legible it will be, especially on larger display type. The reason for this relates to the above rule about not using all capitals: Because viewers recognize shapes of words rather than individual letters, tighter letter spacing helps visually establish the shape of each word. For display type—the larger the type, the more important this is—the designer must "eyeball" it, paying close attention to the space between each letter. On very large type, letter spacing will vary from letter to letter within the same word. Some typographers will cover the bottom half of their display type with a sheet of paper, which helps them better see which letters need adjusting.

A note about terminology: Some computer programs refer to letter spacing as "kerning." Technically, "kerning" is the term used to describe the tightening of letter spacing and "letterspacing" describes loosening. (To "kern" your type is to tighten it, to "letterspace" it is to loosen it. Note that the noun "letter spacing" is two words, while the verb "letterspace" is one word.) However, computer programs and common usage have muddied the use of these terms.

Looser line spacing is more legible. If you have the space to do so, use loose line spacing (or "leading," a term derived from strips of lead once used by typesetters between lines of type on a plate for a printing press). A rule of thumb is that your leading (pronounced like "letting") measurement on body text should be at least two points larger than your type. So 10-point type should be set with a minimum of 12-point leading, 12-point type should have a leading of 14 points or more, etc. If you can be even more generous with your leading, do so. Ten-point type set with a leading of 14 or 16 points is more legible and less cluttered than with 12-point leading. However, don't expand your leading so much that it creates a striping effect. Be sure that the white space between lines of type does not appear to be the same width as the type itself. This sometimes requires printing a proof and looking at it to be sure.

A note about terminology: Typographers refer to point size and leading measurements as follows: 10-point type set with 12-point leading is described as "10 over 12," 24-point type set with 36-point leading is "24 over 36," and so on.

Don't double-space after punctuation. The practice of adding two spaces after periods is a relatively new one in the grand scheme of the timeline of typography. Typography dates back to the 15th century in the West, and considerably further in Asia. The post-period double-space seems to be a relic from the relatively recent days of the typewriter, where monospaced characters (each typographic character taking the same amount of space, be it an M or an I) created such a uniform pattern on the page that the double-space made it easier to recognize a new sentence. However, since computers have given designers control over their typography that far exceeds even that of the printing press, a single space following a period looks far better than two spaces and is the current industry standard.

Use em-dashes, en-dashes, and hyphens appropriately. These three typographic characters look similar but have very different roles. Hyphens are used exclusively for breaking words from one line to the next or combining compound words or phrases. The en-dash, which resembles a hyphen but is slightly longer (the length of the letter "N" in a given character set), is used to indicate duration, as in, "The birdwatching program is scheduled for 11:00 a.m.–2:00 p.m." The em-dash is longer still (the length of the letter "M") and is used where you might otherwise use a colon or parentheses. For instance, "Mendenhall Glacier—along with other ice fields in Alaska—is receding more quickly than ever." Note that there are no spaces between em-dashes and surrounding words. One common typographic mistake is to use two hyphens in place of an em-dash. This is incorrect, and can lead to awkward line breaks.

Use smart quotes. Smart quotes, also known as curly quotes, are so named because they are smart enough to know where they are going. They curl in the appropriate direction to lead the reader into or out of quotations. Dumb quotes, on the other hand, stand straight up and down. Apostrophes should curl as well. Most computer programs automatically place smart quotes and apostrophes, but be sure to check, especially when you are copying and pasting text from one computer program to another. Also, be sure that the computer curls your quotes in the appropriate direction. For instance, when abbreviating a calendar year, the computer will frequently turn quotes inward when they are meant to turn outward. "The years 2007 and '08" is incorrect. It should be "The years 2007 and '08." (Note the direction of the apostrophe in front of "08.")

One instance where dumb quotes and apostrophes are appropriate is when you are abbreviating feet and inches, as in, "The average kangaroo is 5' 2" tall."

■ Smart quotes are smart because they know where they're going.

■ Dumb quotes have no sense of direction.

Avoid Comic Sans!

The use of Comic Sans or its insidious cartoon handwriting cousins is a dead giveaway that an amateur has had his or her hand in a project. While there are rare, specific instances where these typefaces are appropriate (in an actual cartoon, for instance), they look unprofessional and fail to achieve the friendly tone they strive for because they are over-used computer defaults. In fact, Comic Sans is as cold and impersonal as fonts get. It's like thanking a friend with a form letter. Though some argue that Comic Sans achieves an air of informality since it purports to look like handwriting, we recommend that you use a round, friendly sans serif like Frutiger, Verdana, or Tahoma instead. Resist the temptation and avoid Comic Sans!

Parts of a Letterform

The diagram below identifies some of the more common terms that identify parts of a letterform. These terms are useful in discussing the details of typography.

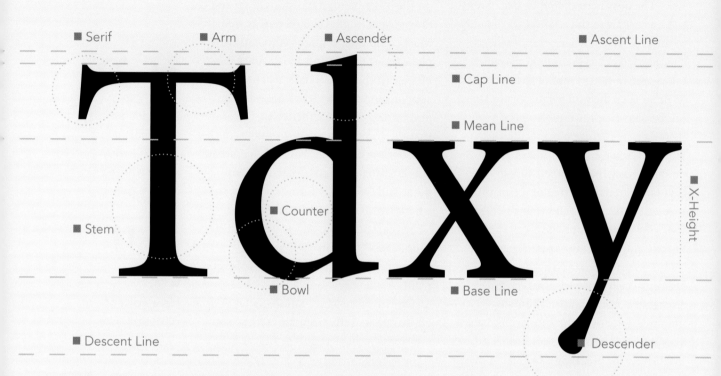

■ **Arm** Horizontal stroke with at least one end that does not connect to another stroke.

■ **Ascender** Stroke that extends above the mean line.

■ **Ascent Line** The point to which ascenders extend in a font. Sometimes extends beyond the cap line.

■ **Base Line** Indicates the lowest part of a letter that does not have descenders.

■ **Bowl** Rounded stroke.

■ **Cap Line** Indicates the top of capital letters in a given font.

■ **Counter** Enclosed portion of a letterform.

■ **Descender** Stroke that extends below the base line.

■ **Descent Line** Point to which descenders extend.

■ **Serif** Flared end of a stroke.

■ **Stem** Primary stroke of a letterform.

■ **Mean Line** Indicates the top of a lower-case letter with no ascender.

■ **X-Height** Measurement from baseline to mean line. Can vary from font to font (making some fonts look larger than others, even at the same point size).

Don't pluralize with apostrophes. Many typographers can't resist the inclination to pluralize certain types of nouns with apostrophes, even though we all learned long ago that this is incorrect. The three most common mistakes in this area deal with decades, capitalized abbreviations, and last names. There is no need for an apostrophe when referencing a decade—the 1990s, for instance (not the 1990's). For some reason, people are uncomfortable with the transition from numerals to letters and want to insert an apostrophe, but you should resist this temptation. Similarly, capitalized abbreviations are regularly mistreated. DVDs and CDs are nouns just like any other and should not be DVD's and CD's. And those neighbors down the road? They're the Smiths, not the Smith's.

Different types of paragraph alignment serve different purposes. Most body text is set either in "flush left/ragged right" (some computers call it "left justified") or "justified." Flush left/ragged right (as the text in this book is set) creates even, consistent letter spacing and word spacing and an organic, inconsistent edge on the right side of the page. One potential pitfall of flush left/ragged right alignment is that long words can lead to large, gaping holes at the end of a line of type. This can usually be mitigated through hyphenation or tightening or loosening of letter spacing. Justified type is flush against the margin on both the left and right sides of the column or page. It creates a uniform, clean look, but can create awkward word or letter spacing issues if there are too few words on a line of text. Centered text and flush right (or "right justified") should be used sparingly for display purposes. They should never be used for entire paragraphs.

- ■ Flush left/ragged right creates even, consistent letter spacing and word spacing and an organic, inconsistent edge on the right side of the column or page.

- ■ Justified type, flush against the margin on both the left and right sides of the column or page, can create word spacing issues.

- ■ Centered text and flush right (or "right justified") should be used sparingly for display purposes.

Photographs

Graphic design can be described as coordinating the interaction of type and image. A single, high-quality image can be the cornerstone of a publication, website, exhibit, sign, or identity system. The National Association for Interpretation's 2006 National Workshop, which featured Route 66 in its logo and slogan, built much of its identity around a photograph provided by the Albuquerque Convention and Visitors Bureau. The photo, consistent with visual elements on the workshop logo, features the neon lights of Route 66 as it passes through the city's downtown, with the Sandia Mountains (also featured in the workshop logo) in the distance. The Route 66 photo found its way onto nearly every workshop publication and was placed prominently on the workshop website.

The color scheme for NAI's 2007 International Conference in Vancouver was built around a single photograph that captured the essence of British Columbia's subdued, peaceful natural setting.

One of the nice things about working with and for interpreters is the preponderance of talented amateur and professional photographers in the field. With a little bit of digging, it is possible to find images of nearly any resource, and many photographers are willing to share their images for little more than a photo credit and recognition of their resource. Advances in digital photography technology, with high-quality cameras producing high-resolution images, have made sharing photos from around the world easier than ever.

If you are willing and able to pay for photographs, the best thing to do is work directly with a professional, especially one who specializes in a specific subject

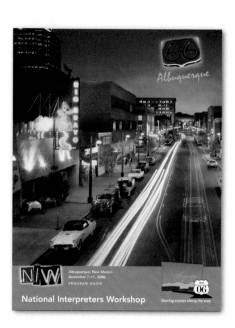

■ The visual identity for NAI's 2006 National Workshop was rooted heavily in this photograph from the Albuquerque Convention and Visitors Bureau.

matter. If time and finances restrict your ability to work with a photographer, there are countless stock photography resources online. An Internet search of the term "stock photography" generates a list of nearly two million sites. (See Chapter 8 for more on resources like stock photography sites.) Note that it is important to be specific about the subject matter of stock photography. It is all too easy to find an image that looks right, but is just slightly off. For instance, a search for an image of the city of Philadelphia's skyline will produce attractive results, but the unwitting designer who purchases a photo taken before February 2007 will have spent a lot of money on an image that does not include the city's tallest building.

Note that it is never a good idea to use just any photograph found on the Internet. Not only are there copyright and intellectual property issues, but most online images are low resolution and will appear pixelated if used for print purposes. (See Chapter 5, "Technical Specifications," for more on resolution and file format issues.)

Once you have found your photograph or photographs, knowing what to do with them is the next step. Entire books have been written about the composition of photographs, but the following basic rules will help you create and compose attractive images.

■ This photograph from Tourism Vancouver established the identity and color scheme of materials for NAI's 2007 International Conference in Vancouver, British Columbia.

■ Rule of thirds: Important visual elements fall on guidelines created by dividing the page into thirds. This photo was taken in British Columbia, Canada.

Rule of thirds: The most well-known rule of composition advises that you divide your image into three equal parts horizontally and vertically. The strongest visual elements in the photograph should be aligned with these imaginary guidelines. This rule also works as a "rule of fifths" with certain images. The most important thing to remember is that the best way to ruin the impact of your image is to center the subject of your photo or the horizon in a landscape.

■ Lines created by architectural elements and the interaction of sunlight and shadows at this hotel in Puerto Morelos, Mexico, draw viewers' eyes to the focal point of the image.

PAUL CAPUTO

Use lines to guide the viewer's eye: Elements like fences, trails, rivers, creeks, or any other features that create a distinct line in an image should be used to draw the viewer's eye to the focal point of the image. A line that guides the viewer's eye away from the intended subject will detract from the quality of the image.

PAUL CAPUTO

PAUL CAPUTO

■ Interesting textures **are** abundant in nature.

Use texture: Extreme cropping techniques can create a dramatic effect. This photo of a giant sequoia taken at Muir Woods National Monument shows a dramatic color palette and uses texture to capture the viewer's attention.

■ This image from Zion National Park's Virgin River creates interest through its use of the unique texture of the water-carved canyon walls.

PAUL CAPUTO

Facing into the frame: Whether you are dealing with video or photos, the subject should lead the viewer's eye to the center of the image rather than to the outer edge. A person who is looking toward the right side of the photo should be on the left side of the image and vice versa. An animal or vehicle that is moving from right to left should be in the right side of the image (moving into the image rather than out of it).

Get some perspective: Look up. Look down. Lie down on your back and shoot toward the sky. Get on your stomach for a worm's-eye view. This will help you find unique angles and create eye-catching photos.

■ This ground squirrel in Rocky Mountain National Park is facing left, so it is largely on the right side of the photo.

■ Changing your vantage point can make for dramatic photos.

RUSSELL DICKERSON

ROGER RIOLO

JAMIE KING

■ Late afternoon light at Red Rock Canyon in Nevada creates dramatic shadows.

Shoot when the sun is low in the sky: You will get the most dramatic effect on landscape photos if you shoot in the early morning or late afternoon, when the low sun creates strong shadows. When the sun is high in the sky during the middle of the day, the light is harsh and shadows are scarce.

■ Depth of field: A distinct plane of focus makes for strong photos, as with this leaf in Rocky Mountain National Park.

Depth of field: Photos that have a subject in sharp focus, while the background and foreground are out of focus, are appealing. This usually requires an SLR (single-lens reflex) camera (as opposed to a "point-and-shoot" camera).

Avoid using a flash: Your camera's automatic flash creates a harsh, unforgiving light that will create unflattering results. If you can introduce enough indirect light through opening windows or turning on indoor lights, the results will be softer and more natural. Remember, though, that most indoor light filaments contain a chemical element called tungsten, which causes photos to have a yellow cast. This effect can be corrected with photo-editing software like Adobe Photoshop.

Found objects: It is the responsibility of designers to be aware of resources that are so obvious they can be overlooked. Just outside our doors lies a world of inspiration, filled with color combinations, organic forms, and even new and inventive typefaces if your neighborhood is, like many, teeming with hand-made flyers for lost pets and weekend yard sales. It's the sort of inspiration one might not find in *Print* magazine or any other professional resource, but it's every bit as important.

Legacy Trust Fund

■ The oak leaf used in the identity for NAI's capital campaign, the Legacy Trust Fund, was picked up off the sidewalk and scanned on a flatbed scanner.

Clip Art is Evil

For the purposes of this discussion, it is important to note that what we refer to as "clip art" is the generic, cartoonish artwork that you find on CDs that come free with inkjet printers or word processing software. While some interpretive illustrators refer to their product as clip art because it can be used generically after purchase, their work is not to be confused with true clip art, which is rarely if ever appropriate for legitimate interpretive communication.

Many interpretive sites do not enjoy the luxury of a budget that allows for paying project-specific illustrators or photographers. However, alternatives to clip art are not as elusive as one might think. First, many people do not consider themselves to be illustrators. But even a person with no artistic skill at all (if such a person truly exists) stands a better chance of effectively conveying the sense of a message or the attitude of an organization than does clip art. Clip art appears everywhere. It was designed to be ambiguous and personality-free so that it might accidentally suit a wide range of unforeseen purposes. Those individuals who venture to create their own illustrations will find that not only do they have access to any image they want (after a couple of minutes with a pen and paper), but that their illustrations take on a certain style, giving their publications a personality that is unique.

Because clip art appears everywhere—and because anyone who has ever been in a room that has a computer in it knows that it's not that hard to place a clip-art file in a word processing document—it has the opposite effect of "sprucing up" a docu-

■ Illustrations like this one by artist Mary Ann Bonnell can bring style and a consistent look to your compositions.

ment. The only story it tells is that of someone who needs to get a newsletter to the printer sitting at a computer and scrolling through a list of 3,000(!) images, looking for the one that comes the closest to saying what he or she wants it to say.

If you don't have access to high-quality illustrations, we recommend using photographic images, which anyone can acquire with a digital camera.

Illustrations

High-quality illustrations are harder to come by than high-quality photos. (On the other hand, low-quality illustrations are extremely easy to come by, although not very useful.) Unless you are lucky enough to know an artist who is willing to dedicate time and effort to help you, the best option is to pay for artwork created by an illustrator. What differentiates illustrations from clip art is the level of expertise of the artist—not just in the quality of the image but also in the subject knowledge of the artist. For interpreters, the National Association for Interpretation's *Interpreter's Green Pages* list a number of illustrators who specialize in subjects as specific as birds, insects, or architecture.

Materials

Suppose you are a volunteer at a rural nature center and you have been assigned the task of designing a brochure that will become the center's primary promotional piece. Your background is in molecular biology, not graphic design or interpretation, but you're the only person in the building who has ever used a computer, so the job is yours.

You've chosen your typefaces—an elegant, organic serif as the primary body text, supported by a clean, bold sans serif to suggest that the center isn't living in the past; it's about progress in the name of nature. You've chosen a color scheme—mostly a soothing, analogous set of greens (of course) but also vivid highlights of bright red—green's complement—to show energy, warmth, and excitement about the resource. You've even persuaded the copywriters to eliminate about half the text they provided in the first draft (beginning with all of the adverbs) so that you could set your leading nice and loose, not just because it's more legible that way, but as a nod to the airy, comfortable feeling visitors will get when they breathe in that fresh, forest air at your site. The photos are perfect, you're thrilled with the layout, and everyone has responded well to the proofs they've seen. You hand over the digital files to the full-time staff, content with a job well done, just before you go off to the annual molecular biology conference in Las Vegas for two weeks.

When you return, you are horrified to find that Meredith, the nature center's well-meaning but out-to-lunch executive director has had the brochure printed on fluorescent pink copy paper (which isn't even recyclable, for crying out loud) because she thought it would catch people's eyes. Just like that, all of your careful work is flushed down the drain. Every good decision you made about how best to represent this site has been undone by one monstrous, irreversible bad decision.

Of course, this is an extreme example, but the choices you make about what materials to use for the final product have as much influence on the message as any other design decision. Some decisions are basic and obvious: Should a wayside exhibit be produced on a high-tech polymer or fastened by bolts to natural wood? Should your site's letterhead be printed on flecked, natural-looking paper or on a bright white matte (which is every bit as recycled and environmentally friendly as the flecked paper)? Other decisions are less obvious, but still heavily influence the user's experience. Should you use a coated matte paper stock or a coated gloss? Should you request a soy-based ink, or are there other environmentally friendly options that are more appropriate for your project?

Types of materials as they relate to specific media will be discussed in later chapters, but the subject is introduced here because it is a basic design decision, and one you should be thinking about before you even begin your initial sketches.

Elements of Composition

Hierarchy

When laying out text and images in any type of media, the first question to ask yourself is, "What do I want my audience to see first?" It could be a single word, a phrase, or an image, but whatever it is, it should clearly be the most prominent element in the composition. If multiple elements compete for status of first-read, then the entire composition loses its punch. One of the quickest ways for a composition to become chaotic and disorganized is when a designer tries to emphasize too much. If too much text on a page is bold or too many images are printed at the largest size possible to draw attention to them, then the page becomes a jumbled mess and the message is lost.

Levels of content can be broken down roughly into three categories:

Primary: This is the attention grabber, the element that draws your audience into the composition. It could be the headline "Man Lands on Moon" or an image of Neil Armstrong on the moon, but it should not be both. Photographs can be effective at this level of hierarchy because they have the potential to be rich visually and convey powerful messages (and they're worth a thousand words, which is about 997 more than you could realistically use at this level of hierarchy if you used actual text).

If you use text as your primary element, it should be limited to three or four words and be set in large, bold type. When text is the first-read, be sure that any images you use are small enough that they do not compete for attention. In a publication, the heaviest and most visually prominent design elements should appear at the inside top of each page spread. (See "Setting Up a Grid" later in this chapter.)

■ These two simple compositions use the same image and the same type. The above example demonstrates the use of image as the primary level of hierarchy, while the example below uses text for its first-read.

Secondary: Supporting text and images make up the bulk of the communication. This is where readers who have been drawn in by the top level of hierarchy come to find out more. The second-read information includes descriptive text, like the body text of a publication and photo captions, or smaller, supporting images on a sign or in an exhibit.

Tertiary: This level includes information like contact information, hours of operation, or instructions on how to find out information for those readers who have been truly engaged by an interpretive product.

In their book *Signs, Trails, and Wayside Exhibits*, Michael Gross, Ron Zimmerman, and Jim Buchholz address hierarchy with the 3–30–3 Rule. They say:

> 3 seconds: Most visitors will look at a sign for 3 seconds. This message usually includes an intriguing title and large graphics.

> 30 seconds: Some visitors who are interested will continue to look at a sign for about 30 seconds. The main message is usually in large letters and about one to two paragraphs long.

> 3 minutes: A few visitors who are interested will look at a sign for up to three minutes. More detailed information and graphics, usually of a smaller size, can be provided for this group.

Contrast

One way of describing how hierarchy is achieved is through contrast. The element on a page that creates the highest degree of contrast is the primary level of hierarchy. Degrees of contrast can be achieved in a number of ways: through size, color palette, shape, or combinations of multiple design elements. Contrast can be achieved even within a single font family using different stroke widths.

The most common way to create contrast is through color. As discussed earlier in this chapter, colors that oppose each other on the color wheel create the strongest contrast. Color combinations like blue and orange, red and green, and yellow and purple create the highest frequency contrast. Similarly, pure black and pure white or different values of a single color create contrast when juxtaposed, either immediately adjacent to one another or one within the other.

Other methods of creating contrast are similarly simple. A large element contrasts with a small element. A rough, organic shape contrasts with a smooth, geometric shape. An inconsistent texture contrasts with a smooth texture.

Regardless of the design element you choose to manipulate to create contrast, the common thread is that only one element changes. It may seem obvious, but, for instance, a large element does not contrast with a blue element (they're simply different, not contrasting). To create contrast, the elements should be similar in every way but the one that creates contrast. A green apple contrasts more effectively with a red apple of similar shape and size than it does with, say, a banana, which is different in many ways.

Another way to think about contrast is by juxtaposing your composition with what your audience is accustomed to seeing. Changing a single element within an otherwise normal setting can jar the visitor into paying attention. For instance, if a visitor to a nature center sees an image of a one-inch-long acorn printed six feet tall, the contrast comes from the visitor's own knowledge of how large an acorn is supposed to be. Making a human face purple or some other unnatural color creates contrast. Printing a single word or even a single letter within a word upside down creates contrast simply because it's unexpected (so long as it's display text and not some random word in the middle of the body of text).

The level of contrast is an essential part of the communication. The more severe the contrast, the more striking the visual communication. This is not to say that the goal is always high contrast. Lack of contrast can be an effective design decision, when implemented with care. Low levels of contrast create a subtle, understated message. As with any design element, know what you want to achieve before you start to lay it out.

Bleeds

Extending a design element (most typically an image or a solid field of color) all the way to the edges of the composition is called "bleeding." Bleeds can extend to one, two, three, or all four edges. (The images on the pages at the beginning of each chapter in this book bleed on three sides—all except for the bottom.) A composition completely covered by an image, texture, or field of color with no margin is call a "full bleed."

If you choose to use bleeds in a printed publication or manufactured piece, be sure to check with your printer or fabricator to see how it will alter your production costs and the specifics of the digital file you will provide. Materials that bleed are generally more expensive to produce. As you prepare your design, be aware that most printers require bleeding elements to extend beyond the boundary of a layout at least an eighth of an inch, and some fabricators require as much as an inch or more to give them some room for error when they trim the final piece.

White Space

White space is sometimes referred to as "negative space," but this seems unnecessarily pessimistic and detracts from the role it plays in the overall layout of your piece. Since white space does not have to actually be white (merely consistent with the background of the rest of the page), another less common but more appropriate term is "counterform." Whatever you call it, white space is usually the first casualty when an inexperienced designer gets hold of a project. However, designers should understand that white space plays a valuable role in a composition and should not be treated as an opportunity to add more content to a page. White space should be treated as a design element that

■ Even using a single typeface in a single color, it is possible to create contrast through differences in scale and stroke width.

■ Complementary colors emphasize contrast.

helps create balance in your layout. It does more than simply make your page attractive, it actually makes your page more legible and increases the chances that your audience will stick around to read what's on the page. Research tells us that the eye gets physically tired reading a page that is saturated with text.

White space can be created on a layout by leaving large areas with no type or image (although it may contain a solid field of color), or by generous leading (line spacing) or margins. Just as the first-person interpreter should avoid inundating visitors by unloading every piece of information he or she has ever learned about a resource during a 30-minute tour, so should designers be aware that their message is much more effective if they limit the amount of information on a page. Cramming every square inch of space on a layout with information will create a cluttered look and result in sensory overload. One of your responsibilities as a designer is to return text to copywriters for editing if there is too much of it.

Historically, one of the most effective uses of white space was the Volkswagen Beetle's classic advertisements created by the advertising and design firm of Doyle Dane Bernbach during the 1950s and 1960s. In an era when most automobile manufacturers were publishing ads that featured full-color images of elaborate vehicles (replete with tailfins and pin-striping) in intricate scenarios, the Bug's understated and timeless campaign helped begin a revolution of public opinion. It was as if a man walked into a room of screaming auctioneers and started speaking in a normal tone of voice. Suddenly, everyone stopped to listen, and a car that had heretofore been looked down upon as ugly, noisy, and unsafe became a cultural phenomenon that continues to this day.

The Designer's Best Friend: A Grid

At this point in the process, you should have selected meaningful and appropriate colors, typefaces, images, and other design elements. You should know which elements will be most prominent in the composition and which will be supporting elements. Most importantly, you should be confident that all of the individual elements that you have assembled support the primary message of your site or organization.

Now comes the time to put everything together. Simply put, graphic design is the synthesis of type and image. Making meaningful information accessible to the audience is the most important job a designer has. The best way to accomplish this is to organize information and design elements in a systematic and consistent way. (Note: Making compositions that are visually appealing is the designer's second-most important role.)

■ **White space helps.** In the 1960s, Volkswagen built an entire advertising campaign with the creative use of white space.

Most of the rules addressed so far are designed not just to reinforce a message, but also to help avoid clutter in a composition. For instance, choosing a color palette keeps us from throwing every color in the rainbow (or Pantone swatch book) into a composition. Limiting a publication to two typefaces prevents us from using every font in the pull-down menu. These rules keep our compositions clean but expressive. The last (and perhaps most important) step in establishing order in a legible and meaningful composition is the use of a simple and flexible grid.

Whether you are designing a one-page flyer or a 200-page book, the most traditional and easy-to-use method to organize information in a useful and visually appealing way is a grid. By aligning design elements to evenly spaced vertical and horizontal guidelines, the designer brings a sense of order to a composition. Without a grid, design elements placed at random or squeezed into open spaces look jumbled and information is difficult to access.

A grid layout that uses vertical and horizontal axes to guide the placement of page elements—also called the International Typographic Style—was popularized in Europe, particularly by the Swiss, in the 1950s. With an emphasis on order, cleanliness, and legibility, the system quickly spread to the United States and Latin America and is now a standard of page composition. The classic text *Grid Systems in Graphic Design* (1961) by Swiss typographer and teacher Josef Müller-Brockmann (1914–1996) compiles decades of wisdom on the subject.

Setting Up a Grid

Determining the specifications of your grid does not take long, and the template you come up with will serve you for as long as you choose to use it. The following process will guide you through establishing a five-column format for an 8" x 10" publication (like this book), but it can be applied to any size publication or sign (or a single sheet) with as many columns as you choose to use. While five columns may seem like a lot for a publication that is only eight inches wide, note that design elements can span more than one column. So, since a single column may be too narrow for traditional body text, columns of text will span two or three columns on the grid. This will leave one or two columns on each page for photo captions, pull quotes, or small images.

Margins: The first step will be to set up margins. Typographic conventions suggest that the margin on the bottom of the page should be larger than the top margins, sometimes by as much as two times. Likewise, outside margins (near the outer edges of the page) should be larger than inside margins (near the binding between pages). On this page, the top margin is 35 points and the bottom margin is 54 points; the inside margin is 44 points and the outside margin is 56 points. These numbers may seem arbitrary now, but they'll make sense soon. (Most software allows you to choose the unit of measurement for your documents. One inch equals 72 points.)

Note that if your composition is something other than a publication with facing pages, there are no inside and outside margins, just left and right. In this instance, the left and right margins should be equal, but the rule still holds that the top margin should be smaller than the bottom margin.

The origins of this convention date back to early printing presses. Publications were (and still are) printed on large sheets that contained four, eight, or 16 pages. These large sheets, called signatures, were folded and cut to create individual pages after they were printed. Because the

■ The margins on this page are highlighted. Note that the top margin is smaller than the bottom margin, and the inside margin is smaller than the outside margin.

devices used to cut the signatures were not always precise, early typographers concentrated the most important information on the inside and top of page spreads, while most of the white space occurred on the outer and bottom edges, where most of the cutting takes place. This convention continues to this day, and as a culture, our eyes are trained to look for the heaviest and most important information on the inside and top of each page spread.

Columns: Columns represent half of a grid, the vertical axes.

Columns help designers organize type and images using vertical guidelines. They define margins on the left and right sides of a composition. In publications, they define the inside margin, the space between pages that includes the fold. A composition with an odd number of columns (typically three or five) is more visually appealing and gives the designer more flexibility than a composition with an even number of columns (two or four). Since design elements can stretch across multiple columns, the more columns a composition has, the more options a designer has.

As noted, this publication contains five columns. The width between columns, the gutter, is 14 points. So, with four 14-point gutters, and inside and outside margins that account for 100 points, that leaves us 420 points to be divided equally over five columns. Thus, each column is 84 points. Note that these numbers were carefully considered not just for their aesthetics and to follow all of the pertinent layout protocols, but also to keep decimal points out of the grid. A change of a single point for a margin or gutter width would leave us dealing with measurements like 84.3 points, which are simply cumbersome. Try to deal with whole numbers (or simple fractions if you're working in inches) whenever possible.

Horizontal guides: The other half of the grid is a series of at least three (usually more) evenly spaced horizontal axes. Though less obvious than the vertical axes, these guidelines are essential in establishing hierarchy and consistency not just in a single composition, but throughout a publication or in a series of compositions.

The heaviest items hang from the same horizontal axis (Axis A). This is called the primary axis (usually at the top of the page out of necessity) and should contain the heaviest and most important visual elements throughout the publication. Axis B contains secondary information and Axis C contains tertiary information. Note that to complete the effect of creating horizontal lines across the page spread, design elements (be they text blocks or images) must appear on the axes on both pages of the page spread. Once the primary axes have visual elements placed on them, use the other axes to guide the placement of additional items (as with the note on the bottom right of the opposite page).

Horizontal guidelines don't just help you align elements (essential to clean design), but they inform the placement of text and images so that similar elements appear at about the same place on every page. If an axis is used for photo captions throughout a publication (or a series of signs, exhibits, or any other composition), the reader will quickly learn where to look for that information. Your compositions will develop a consistent look that helps build an identity, making information that much easier to access, and your design, by extension, that much more effective.

Once you have set up the grid, using it is simple. The tops of design elements should hang from horizontal guides (rather than having their bottoms rest on them). Likewise, the left side of each design element should align with the left

■ **Horizontal guidelines** help organize information in a publication. Flip through this book and you'll notice captions and other items in the outside columns usually fall on Axis B, beginning 161 points from the top of the page.

■ **This caption** spans one column. The blocks of body text on this page span two columns, while the block of body text on the opposite page spans three columns. This type of grid allows for flexibility and consistency.

■ What separates professionals from amateurs? **The grid! Note how the top of each item on this page hangs from a horizontal gridline and the left side aligns with a vertical guide. However, the bottoms of text blocks or images do not need to rest on a gridline, nor do the right sides of these items need to land exactly on a vertical guide.**

side of a column (the right side does not necessarily have to align with a guideline). So, while the grid dictates the placement of the top left corner of each item, the bottom right corner should fall simply where the design element ends. That is, if one column of text descends three or four lines beyond another, that's okay. If one photo is taller or wider than another, no problem, provided that the top and/or left edges line up with other elements on the page. This allows for a composition to maintain an organic, fluid look while still being organized.

Note that when you are establishing the location of your horizontal gridlines, be sure that they fall in such a way that when you hang traditional body text from different guidelines, the base lines of lines of text line up across columns. To do this, your horizontal gridlines should be placed at a measurement that is a multiple of your leading (this text is set with 14-point leading and there are nine lines of text between gridlines, so the gridlines are 126 points apart; nine multiplied by 14 is 126).

■ Note how the baselines of this text and the body text line up. This helps keep your layout clean.

■ **The distance between each** horizontal guide is 126 points— equal to nine lines of text at 14-point leading.

■ 126 Points

Rules are Made to Be Broken

The worst reason to break any of the rules or guidelines discussed above is that you do not know the rule in the first place. The best reason to break any of the above rules is that you know the rule, but believe that you can communicate more strongly by breaking it. As soon as you learn any rule about color usage, typography, and imagery, you will find reasons to break it. Nonpersonal interpretive media would be incredibly boring if every designer followed the same set of rules to the letter all of the time. As with any design decision, the only criteria are that you know what you're doing and why you're doing it. Be able to defend your decisions and explain how those decisions improve the communication you create. (See "When to Break the Rules" in Chapter 7 for more on this.)

■ Opposite page: Azaleas in the Hamarikyu Garden in Tokyo.

From Pre-press to Production

Once you have decided how your project is going to look, it's important that you know how to set up your files, choose the appropriate software, and work with your printer to achieve the final output that you expect (and deserve) after putting so much time and thought into your composition. This chapter discusses preparing image files, the role of various types of popular computer programs, and soliciting price quotes from print-ers, in that order. However, it is by no means a strictly sequential process. You may start by calling several printers for some basic information (like what resolution they expect your image files to be or the most cost-efficient size for your project) before you even turn on the computer, or you may set up a template in page-layout software before you start working with images. Most likely, you will work with the three important parts of the process discussed in this chapter simultaneously.

Technical Specifications

Preparing Image Files

One very important step in creating professional-quality design products is using the correct format and resolution for your images. Nothing flags a publication as amateurish more quickly than jagged, pixelated, or fuzzy images. The notes below will guide you in selecting the correct file format and preparing image files.

Resolution

Digital image files can be divided into two very important categories: those for print media and those for screen (Web, video, or other projected media). The most important distinctions are in resolution (dots per inch or pixels per inch) and color mode (See "Color on the Computer" on the page). The typical resolution of an image prepared for screen media is 72 pixels per inch (or ppi), whereas images prepared for print are usually 300 dots per inch (dpi). Sometimes, especially in large-format printed pieces like signs or exhibits, the resolution can be lower than 300 dpi. Check with the folks who will be producing the final piece before getting started.

Note that an image that is 72 pixels per inch is the same resolution as an image at 72 dots per inch. The reason for the differentiation lies in how the image will ultimately be used. Pixels per inch is used for screen images and dots per inch is used for print. Practically speaking, the only difference between the two is that a pixel (on screen) is square and a dot (on the printed page) is round.

This difference in resolution is why images pulled directly from a website look terrible when they are placed in a printed document. Most computer monitors only project at 72 dots per inch, so images saved at a higher resolution simply cause longer download times without the benefit of added quality. Because images prepared for the Web sacrifice image quality in favor of a smaller, Web-friendly file size, they are almost always too low resolution to use in printed materials.

So, when you're looking for an image for your printed newsletter and you hear, "Oh, sure, we have a picture of that. Just grab it off our website," ask instead for a high-resolution digital file or an original print or slide to scan. Many agencies and sites offer high-resolution images for download from special media sections of their websites. Often, these sites are accessible to the public or simply require a quick phone call or e-mail to a media relations person at the site.

■ Resolution matters! The top photo of our friend Iguana "Don" is saved at 300 dots per inch, appropriate for most print media. Below, he's saved at 72 dots per inch (as you would find on the Internet).

Color on the Computer

Working with color on the computer can be a frustrating endeavor even for the most seasoned professional. Colors as they appear on computer monitors are created by light frequencies while colors on printed materials are based on pigments or inks. This difference alone, not to mention that different computer programs on the same machine handle colors differently, can mean that what you see on your screen is going to look different from what's printed. When you're working with a professional printing press, it's somewhat easier to achieve the color you desire (see PMS colors below). If you're using a home or office laser or inkjet printer, the best you can do is learn the quirks of your hardware through trial and error. Below are some basic terms that will help you understand color on your computer:

RGB stands for red, green, and blue, and refers to the light frequencies that create images on screens and monitors. Combinations of these three light frequencies can create an extremely wide array of colors. If you're working strictly in an on-screen medium, like the Web or video, this is an advantage. If you're designing a piece to be printed, what you see on screen is likely brighter and richer than what the final printed product will look like.

CMYK stands for cyan, magenta, yellow, and black, and refers to the pigments used in printed materials. (The K stands for black to avoid confusion with the B for blue in RGB.) Combinations of these four pigments can create a wide array of colors, though not as wide as RGB. Most computer layout and design programs have an artificial CMYK mode that approximates on screen what a piece will look like when it's printed.

The Pantone Matching System (PMS) is an international standard for creating thousands of specific colors, usually for printed materials. You can purchase a swatch book with thousands of numbered PMS colors that will print exactly the same whether your printing press is local or in Singapore. When you design a one- or two-color piece, designate spot colors using your PMS swatch book and you can't go wrong.

Grayscale refers to black and white with shades of gray, while the terms bitmap or lineart usually refer to black and white only, with no shading of any kind.

■ RGB color mode is used for on-screen or projected media.

■ CMYK color mode is used for printed media.

PAUL CAPUTO

■ Grayscale images include a full spectrum of grays from white to black, as with this photo of Japan's Lake Chuzenji.

File Formats for Print Purposes

Using the appropriate file format will help your images look as good as they possibly can. Images for print are based on either pixels or vectors (mathematical paths).

Pixel-based images (also called "continuous-tone" images) include photographs, fine art, or other images that may include soft edges or subtle color gradations. They are a finite size because they contain a finite number of pixels. (The more pixels the file contains, the larger the potential print size.) Using image manipulation software (like Photoshop), you can zoom all the way in and look at individual pixels magnified many times over and see the building blocks of this type of image. The standard format for this type of image is TIFF (Targeted Image File Format). Other pixel-based file formats for print include BMP (Bitmap, used mostly for black-and-white images) or PICT (Picture), but TIFF is the most commonly used. These files are typically created on programs like Adobe Photoshop, Adobe Photoshop Elements, or the GNU Image Manipulation Program (GIMP).

So, if you are preparing a color photograph for print, you will get the best image quality by saving it as a TIFF in CMYK color mode at 300 dpi. JPEGs are not appropriate for use in print. If you have a JPEG, resave it as a TIFF before going to print.

Vector-based images include logos, illustrations, or other images that contain only sharp edges or computer-generated gradients (a blend from one color to another color). Vector-based images require a certain amount of expertise to create (the ubiquitous pen tool can be frustrating to learn, but it is invaluable once you have it down), but they have some distinct advantages when you're dealing with a certain type of image. Rather than being based on pixels, each line, shape, or field of color is determined by a mathematical formula or path. (Don't worry, you don't have to know advanced mathematics to create vector-based images; the computer will do it for you.) Vectors eliminate the need to worry about resolution and allow you to print images as large or as small as you like. The same vector-based image could be printed on a business card or a six-foot banner with no quality loss or increase in file size. The standard file format for vector-based images is an EPS (Encapsulated Post Script).

In addition to a smaller file size and freedom from resolution concerns, one advantage of vectors over pixels is that EPS files allow you to have transparent backgrounds, so you can place an EPS logo or illustration on top of a pixel-based photograph or solid field of color.

TIM MERRIMAN

■ Pixel-based or "continuous tone" images like this photo from Tanzania have subtle gradations from one color to the next. For print purposes, save these as TIFFs. For on-screen use, save them as JPEGs.

Another advantage of vector-based EPS files is that they allow you to convert all of your type elements to vectors (sometimes called paths). This means that when you have created a final image that includes type (like a logo), you can convert all of the type to paths and the computer will treat it as it does the rest of the image. This eliminates any concern about whether your printer has the appropriate fonts on their computers, and you can be certain that the final printed product will look like what you're expecting.

Note that the software you use to create EPS files (typically Adobe Illustrator or CorelDRAW) will allow you to embed pixel-based images in your vector-based image. This does not automatically convert your pixel-based image to vectors (nor would you want it to). This simply creates a hybrid image that contains both vectors and pixels. This is a useful function, but if you ask someone for a vector-based version of their logo, be sure that they haven't simply resaved a TIFF or worse, a low-resolution JPEG, as an EPS.

If you have created a logo or other image with sharp edges for print, you will get the best image quality by saving it as a vector-based EPS with fonts converted to paths in CMYK mode.

Files for Screen or Projected Media

The most common file format for images on the Web is the JPEG or JPG, which gets its name from the Joint Photographic Experts Group, which established the standard guidelines for compressing photographs, fine art, or other images that may include soft edges or subtle color gradations—the same types of images that would be saved as TIFFs in a print document. The main advantage of the JPEG is its compression, which creates smaller file sizes and therefore faster loading times for images online or even in a multimedia presentation (like PowerPoint). While the technology continually improves, the main disadvantage is that there is some quality loss when you save an image in this format. The quality of your image will degrade every time you open a JPEG and resave it as a JPEG. For this reason, if you are working with an image that is destined for screen use, it is best to keep a version that is saved as another format that does not compress images (like TIFF or the native format of whatever software you're using, like PSD for Photoshop) and wait until it is in its final form to save it as a JPEG. JPEGs can be created in many programs, most notably Adobe Photoshop, Adobe Fireworks, Adobe Illustrator, CorelDRAW, and GIMP.

If you are preparing a photograph for use on the Web or in a multimedia presentation, you will get the best image quality by saving it as a JPEG in RGB color mode at 72 ppi.

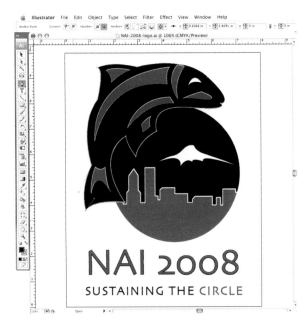

■ Illustration programs use vectors to create images with solid fields of color, like this logo for the 2008 NAI National Workshop (shown here in an Adobe Illustrator window). Note the little blue "handles" on the fish's tail—these are used to manipulate paths in this software.

Save files composed exclusively of solid fields of color as EPS files for print, GIF for screen or projected use.

■ File formats matter! The image on the far right (destined for use on a website) was saved as a GIF when it should have been saved as a JPEG, as it is in the image on the left. Note the lack of subtle color gradations in the GIF.

File Formats at a Glance

Print

TIFF (300 dpi, CMYK color mode):
For "continuous-tone" images
(photos, paintings, etc.)

EPS (vector, CMYK color mode):
For images with solid fields of color
(logos, lineart illustrations, etc.)

Screen/Projected

JPEG (72 ppi, RGB color mode):
For "continuous-tone" images
(photos, paintings, etc.)

GIF (72 ppi, index color mode):
For images with solid fields of color
(logos, lineart illustrations, etc.)

Another common file format for images on the Web is GIF (Graphic Interchange Format). Like EPS files (but for the Web instead of print), GIFs are most appropriate for images with sharp edges and no blending between colors, like logos or some illustrations. Also like EPS images, GIFs allow for transparent backgrounds. Unlike EPS files, GIFs are pixel-based rather than vector-based, so be sure you're working at 72 pixels per inch if you're preparing a GIF. Also unlike EPS files, GIFs can be saved in an animated format. (Another less common file format with similar functionality to GIFs is the PNG, which stands for Portable Network Graphics.)

GIFs use a relatively simple type of compression called Lempel Zev Welch (LZW), which reduces files to include only the specific colors used in the image—with a maximum of 256 colors. Thus, the color format is neither RGB nor CMYK, but rather "index," which is the only color format you can save a GIF in. GIFs are most often created in Adobe Photoshop or Adobe Fireworks.

You have likely seen an image saved as a GIF that should have been saved as a JPEG. For instance, a sunrise that should feature a smooth gradation from the sun to the edges of a photo appears like rings around a planet instead when saved as a GIF. When used appropriately, the GIF will give you a clean image at a low file size, but it is easy to identify when the GIF format has been misused.

If you are preparing a logo or other image with large fields of solid colors for the Web or other projected media, your best bet is a GIF in indexed color mode at 72 ppi.

Software

It is important to remember that the computer is a tool. It is there to help you realize your creative vision, not to shape it. Each piece of software comes with its own bells and whistles, which makes it all too easy to fall into the trap of relying on the software to "jazz up" your design. As with all decisions, be prepared to defend the meaning even—or perhaps especially—of the bells and whistles, such as animated transitions in PowerPoint or easily recognizable filters or effects in Photoshop.

The types of software associated with nonpersonal media can loosely be divided into the following six categories.

Publication and Page Layout

QuarkXPress and Adobe InDesign are the industry standards for multiple-page documents. They can also be used for sign production or exhibit panels. While both programs continue to add features and functionality with each version, they are essentially intended for the arrangement and composition of text and images that have been created using other software. They allow you to set up page templates, including guidelines for margins and grids, and both allow for sophisticated and detailed manipulation of text.

The ultimate product of using either program is a document (or documents) that can be sent directly to a printer for production. These programs allow you to send your original files to a printer or you can generate a PDF (Portable Document Format). Sending the original files keeps the document in an editable state, but it requires that you send the layout document (in Quark or InDesign) as well as all of the individual files for images and fonts that you used in the document. Both Quark and InDesign have easy-to-use commands that collect these files for you.

The debate over which of the two programs is superior has been raging for some time and promises to continue. Quark has been around longer— since 1987 for Macintosh users, 1992 for the PC—and was long considered the uncontested industry standard, the smarter, more talented older brother to the now defunct Aldus Pagemaker. Adobe InDesign was introduced in 2002 and is bundled with other powerful Adobe design software like Photoshop and Illustrator (see below). Ultimately, it's a matter of designer preference or the preference of the production house that determines which program to choose.

Microsoft Publisher performs many of the same functions, but is less technical than QuarkXPress and Adobe InDesign, and is not widely used by professionals. (Many print shops will not accept Publisher documents.) If you're using Publisher, be sure it's for something you're printing in-house.

Photo Retouching and Image Manipulation/Creation

By far, the industry standard in correcting and retouching photographs, manipulating existing images, or creating original digital art is Adobe Photoshop. Released by Adobe Systems in 1990 for the Macintosh (then two years later for the PC), it is without parallel the most powerful and multilayered program in the industry. Its most basic and useful functions include the ability to retouch damaged photographs, as well as adjust highlights and shadows, color balance, and contrast in photographs. Nearly all scanned prints and slides, as well as most digital photographs, need some sort of correction. Photoshop's more complicated and in-depth features—including photo collaging (the realistic combination of

■ Before and after: With its most basic functions, Photoshop can be used to correct color casts (as above), as well as to sharpen or retouch photos.

elements from multiple photographs), the creation of original art, and three-dimensional rendering, just to name a few—continue to expand with each new version. Photoshop can be used to create nearly any type of image file format for any type of medium.

For those interested in learning more about Photoshop and other Adobe products, the National Association of Photoshop Professionals (www.photoshopuser.com) holds biannual conventions and provides a number of training resources for members. Adobe Systems (www.adobe.com) also offers training—much of it free.

Other programs used for photo retouching and original art include Adobe Photoshop Elements (a less expensive, less powerful version of Photoshop) and the GNU Image Manipulation Program (GIMP), a surprisingly good free program found online at www.gimp.org.

Illustration/Logo Design
Adobe Illustrator (first released in 1987 for the Macintosh, 1989 for the PC) and CorelDRAW (released in 1989) are the two most common programs used for creating and manipulating vector-based images, typically EPS files. Both are powerful and widely used. Some professionals prefer CorelDRAW because, in their view, it is more intuitive and less technical than Illustrator, while others prefer Illustrator because of its ability to integrate easily with other Adobe products like Photoshop, InDesign, and Flash, among others. Adobe sells its software in a package called the Creative Suite, so designers who use one Adobe product frequently end up using others as well.

PDF
Any of the above programs for use in print publications will allow you to save your file as a PDF (Portable Document Format). This brilliant file format lets designers share layout proofs or final printable documents without requiring others to have specific software or fonts on their computers. A PDF can be saved with extreme file compression so that entire full-color publications can be posted online at a relatively small file size, or with no compression and with crop marks and full bleeds so that they can be used as the final file provided to a professional printer. The PDF has the advantage of being a single file, but it is more difficult for a printer to make corrections to a PDF if mistakes are found in a proof.

As technology improves, PDFs are becoming increasingly interactive, with the potential for embedding not just static text and image, but video and three-dimensional renderings. Nearly all computers come ready to read PDFs, but in the rare case that one needs software, Acrobat Reader is an easy and free download at www.adobe.com.

Websites
There are many programs called HTML editors available to design and build websites. Adobe Dreamweaver is a powerful and user-friendly option for beginning and advanced designers. It offers a graphic interface so that you can see what the page will look like as you are building it without having to deal with writing any code (although you can if you want to). Learning to build a simple website with text, images, and links in Dreamweaver does not take long, so you can get up and running relatively quickly after reviewing the built-in tutorial, but as with many programs, it is multilayered and has many

features that you will continue to learn over months and years. Other programs include Microsoft Expression Web (formerly Microsoft FrontPage) and a host of free programs available online.

Designing for the Web offers a world of opportunity for the more technically savvy and adventurous. Beyond simple sites lie more complicated bells and whistles like database-driven sites, forums and blogs, various types of scripting, and much, much more.

Multimedia and Video

Microsoft PowerPoint, part of the Microsoft Office suite, is the Kleenex of multimedia presentations. That is, PowerPoint has become so ubiquitous that no one ever says they're doing a slide show or a presentation; instead, they're doing a PowerPoint. First released for the Macintosh in 1987 (then in 1990 for the PC), PowerPoint has become the standard for making simple multimedia presentations using text, images, and sometimes video files because it is easy to use and features templated slide compositions and effects. (See "Design for Presentations and Programs" in Chapter 6 for a discussion of the best use of PowerPoint's features.) While PowerPoint is available for both Mac and PC users, Mac also offers a similar program called Keynote as part of its iWork suite.

Both Mac and PC users can create high-quality videos using relatively simple software. Apple introduced iMovie in 1999, allowing users to easily download and edit digital video and photographs. The software allows for simple transitions, the addition of typographic elements like titles and captions, and the so-called "Ken Burns effect" for still images (named for the documentarian who made famous slow pans and zooms on photographs). The Microsoft Windows operating system includes a similar program called Windows Movie Maker, introduced in 2000.

Other multimedia software for more advanced purposes include Adobe Flash (for creating interactive elements or games for websites or animations for video or online), Adobe Director (for creating animations or interactive elements, frequently for stand-alone media like CD-ROMs or interactive kiosks), and Adobe AfterEffects (a powerful program used for animating graphic elements in film or video).

All of the above multimedia software takes time and energy to master, but if you plan to work extensively with building websites, interactive presentations, or video, they are well worth learning.

Competitive Bidding

During the course of a year, you can expect to work with a variety of different printers or fabricators. For every project you produce, you should solicit an absolute minimum of three bids. You might want to consider a local print house for letterhead, envelopes, business cards, and other small projects, while some of your larger publications may be printed at a distance. For some projects, even going out of country may offer better pricing or quality of product.

The driving force behind the competitive bidding process, of course, is cost. But the ultimate benefit is quality. By soliciting bids on every project you do, you can drive your costs down, and often print a nicer product for less money. (For instance, one printer may be able to offer full color for the same price another can only offer two colors.) You must balance these two factors of price and quality when considering your selection of production house, remembering always that the lowest bid isn't always the best choice when it comes to representing the quality of your organization.

Getting bids for every project keeps you from falling into a rut with production. Feeling that you know which jobs will be printed with which printer before you even begin the project is a surefire way to let costs creep up without you realizing it. Also, as annoying as it may be to interrupt your day, if you do a lot of printing or production, always accept calls from new salespeople wanting to bid on projects. You never know when that perfect match is going to come along.

To avoid instigating a time-consuming bidding war, tell sales representatives that you will award the project based on their first bid. This achieves two important results. First, it maintains a level of professionalism in the process. Second, it assures that you will get the best price a print house can offer on its first bid.

The end result of the competitive bidding process is that your organization will have more money, nicer products, and an armful of salespeople who know that if they don't give you their best bid on their first try, they won't get the job.

■ Take a tour. Many printers, like Modern Litho in Jefferson City, Missouri, will offer a tour of their facilities, where you can get an idea of their level of expertise and the quality of their equipment.

How to Solicit Bids

Production houses or fabricators will ask for information on the following specifications when bidding on a project. Use these specifications as appropriate for printed publications or fabricated exhibits or signs.

Title: If you produce a large number of pieces over the course of the year, this is important information for keeping track of quotes as they come in.

Quantity: The more you print or produce, the cheaper the unit cost. Ask for quotes on multiple quantities (for example, 5,000, 7,500, and 10,000) and compare unit costs for publications or duplicate signs.

Trim Size: Traditional paper sizes have been established to reduce wasted paper and costs when printing publications. Typical sizes include 6" x 9"(for paperback books), 8.5" x 11" (for magazines), and 11" x 17" (tabloid). Depending on the printer and the project, these dimensions may vary slightly. Typical sign sizes are 24" x 36" for horizontal formats or 36" x 48" for vertical formats, but most sign materials can easily be custom-cut without additional cost.

Page Count: When printing publications, strive for multiples of 16 pages to reduce costs. If this is impossible, multiples of eight and four also work. A "signature" is 16 pages. Page counts can include the cover (if the cover is printed on the same paper stock, called a "self cover") or be separate from the cover (if the cover is printed on a heavier stock, called "plus cover").

Inks: Typical ink specifications are four-color (cyan, magenta, yellow, and black—also called full color), two-color (either black plus one spot color or two spot colors), or black only. A publication may have different ink specifications for different pages. For example, a tri-fold brochure that is full color on the outside and black and white on the inside would be described like this: four color over black, or "4C/black."

Paper Stock/Materials: When printing publications, you have a choice of gloss, matte, or offset finishes. Gloss and matte are typical for most high-end print jobs. Offset is like typing paper. You can also choose a weight, typically from 60 lb. (like most magazines) to 100 lb. (thicker paper, usually for shorter publications or brochures). Be specific if the cover stock is different from the interior stock. (See Chapter 6 for information on specific materials used for producing exhibits or signs.)

Bindery: This describes how multiple-page publications are fastened. Saddlestitch (stapled, like a magazine), perfect bound (with a spine, like a paperback book), or casebound (hardback) are typical.

Special Instructions: Use this space to identify if there are special folds, die-cuts, varnishes, or delivery needs.

■ If you solicit bids regularly, set up an e-mail template or word processing document with these specifications. Whenever you need a quote, plug in the new information and send it to every printer in your address book.

■ Opposite page:
Map and interpre-
tive sign at Denali
National Park in
Alaska.

A story of one of the most valuable diamonds ever sold tells of a sale that nearly didn't happen. A wealthy entrepreneur heard of the acquisition and possible sale of a rare diamond in Chicago. The entrepreneur immediately flew to Chicago to see the diamond and to make a decision about buying it. The broker who was responsible for selling it was able to describe all of the technical details of the diamond as well as its complete history. After a detailed presentation, the entrepreneur decided not to buy it. Before he left, though, the diamond's owner asked if he could show him the diamond once again. He held the diamond to the light, described its beauty, and related its value to the importance to him. The owner revealed how the diamond stood out from every other diamond in the world. The entrepreneur purchased it without hesitation. The broker later asked the owner how he made the sale. The owner said, "Simple. You know everything there is to know about diamonds, but I love them."

When designing interpretive media, we shouldn't forget our passion for the places where we work, and the stories that we tell

Special Considerations for Specific Applications

must inspire us. If passion is left out of our materials, then our visitors will never be inspired to learn more on their own. As interpreters it is our job to reveal and relate through the specific applications that we are producing.

Site Publications Plan

A site publications plan or graphic design standards manual helps you identify purpose, direction, and messages across the various media you produce for a specific agency or site. It helps create consistency not only in the look and feel of your nonpersonal media, but also in the message and identity you wish to convey. The process of developing this plan is often more difficult than the implementation. Getting group approval for a consistent design approach requires thoughtful facilitation and ongoing effort. The National Park Service's *Information Design* training manual recommends that all staff involved with publications at a given site meet regularly to make sure everyone is on the same page. An effective site publication plan includes the site mission; site themes; essential experiences at the site; connections to master plan, business plan, interpretive plan, and budget; a complete list of nonpersonal media currently being offered at the site; a complete list of publications used by the site but produced by an outside agency or group; a complete list of proposed publications to be produced; and a complete list of potential publication ideas. A well-designed site publication plan will inform decisions you make about the media discussed below.

Design for Presentations and Programs

Interpretive programs can sometimes be enhanced through visual aids or audio-visual equipment. The use of over-head transparencies, slides, and presentation software like PowerPoint can engage visitors, support topics and themes, and inspire the visitor to learn more. In *Environmental Interpretation*, Sam Ham writes, "What seems clear ... is that the effectiveness of any visual aid has a lot to do with the skill of the person using it." Poor or careless use of these programs or audio-visual equipment will destroy the connection of the visitor to the resource being interpreted. It is important to remember that PowerPoint was created for the corporate world for those who lacked presentation skills and needed a way to present information. Interpreters are not in a typical corporate environment and usually do not lack presentation skills. But seeing the potential offered by the medium, interpreters have been able to use the software to create powerful programs.

PowerPoint's greatest attribute lies in its potential to produce

■ Tips to improve PowerPoint Presentations

Be original. Avoid templates.

Incorporate original images and textures.

Keep it short. Use text sparingly.

Use sans-serif typefaces. Avoid decorative fonts.

Limit to two typefaces.

Change line spacing for impact and readability.

Use color with care. (Bright, warm colors are hard on the eyes when projected.)

Focus on content. Avoid bells and whistles that don't relate.

Be consistent.

multimedia programming to support the interpreter's presentation. In one program, you can add audio tracks, music, photos, text, video, animation, colors, Internet access, links to other programs, and more. Images can be added to a program with ease and the overall development of a presentation can be accomplished quickly through pre-created templates. There are no complicated computer languages to learn. For those who have trouble organizing their thoughts, presentation software can feel like a long-lost friend. Slides can be created and moved to any point in the program with a simple click, drag, and drop. Once a presentation is created, it can be saved in formats for print, slide, or websites, or simply used as an outline to help the interpreter practice his or her presentation.

With all of these positive attributes, it is easy to forget that presentation software should support and not distract from the presenters themselves—as is the case for any prop used in a program. Many of the positive attributes of PowerPoint can quickly become negatives. These programs are easy to use for those with little design experience. However, some who use this medium would be better off presenting through more traditional methods. Since PowerPoint and similar software is readily available, widely used, and easy to learn, some torturous, themeless programs have been developed that are more sizzle than steak.

The linear nature of these presentations—slides in a pre-arranged, sequential order—can be a negative. In presentation mode, there is only one way through the program and that is in a straight line. This linear approach leaves little room for flexibility or allowing for impromptu discussions that may arise during any program. Other buttons and links can be used to

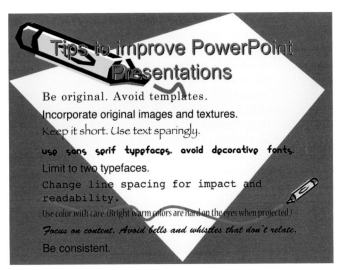

■ Bad PowerPoint slides use templates, rely heavily on text, are bright red, and are generally cluttered. This slide becomes especially offensive if the presenter reads it aloud word for word.

■ Good PowerPoint slides use large, original images, and offer only enough text to support the presenter (without trying to say everything).

achieve nonlinear approaches but require a significant investment of time to learn to use well.

Templates can stamp a program as unprofessional. You don't have to see many multimedia shows before you start to recognize the standardized templates that come with the program. Templates sap programs of their originality and make the otherwise unique voices of interpreters generic and bland.

When creating presentations, multi-media software allows for the mixing of colors and textures. High-contrast complements like blue and orange may resonate so much as to be difficult to look at, as can a stark black on white. More subdued, low-contrast color schemes (like analogous or monochromatic, as discussed in Chapter 4) work better projected or on screen. Similarly, black type should be set against a warm gray or other light color, never against a stark white background. A better choice would be a dark background with lighter type. In any case, check the color contrast in the room you will be using so that you can be sure the light level shows your work to its best advantage.

As presentation software becomes more common, it seems there's a competition to see who can create the most whiz-bang show using the most special effects. Along the way, interpretive principles get lost and presentations become more about software capabilities than the message. Remember that the most important part of any program is the theme—not your proficiency with the software.

One of the most distracting elements of presentation software can be the entrance and exit of text and images. Animation schemes created for these entrances were intended to add emphasis to portions of text. These elements usually include audio accompaniment such as laser beam sounds and typewriter noises that may be "cute" the first time, but rapidly come to grate on audiences' nerves.

The interaction of type and image should be handled with care. If text is placed over a photo, is should be located in an area of the photo with a consistent color in the background, never over a mottled background. Use text sparingly with a few bulleted phrases on one slide rather than several complete sentences. Quotations or other information projected on screen should be referenced but never read aloud.

As with any print media, use caution in the fonts or typefaces that you choose. Sans-serif typefaces such as Arial or Helvetica are easy to read and are good to use in these programs. Avoid using special effects such as drop shadows. Also take into consideration size of the font and the location on the slide to improve readability. If it is at the extreme top, bottom, right, or left on a slide it may not be easily seen by the entire audience. A 30-point typeface should be considered the minimum size for most presentations.

Advantages and Disadvantages of PowerPoint	
Advantages	Disadvantages
Multimedia (audio, video, Web pages, photos) in one location	Cost of equipment
Easy to use	Too linear (impedes spontaneity during presentations)
Organizes information	Templates squelch originality
Supports presenter	PowerPoint "competition"
Transferable format to print, slide, Web	Bells and whistles can be distracting
	Replaces (instead of reinforces) presentation skills

Newsletters

Newsletters are essential management tools. Newsletters are typically used to communicate an organization's mission and update a specific audience of news events. In the book *Layout Index,* Jim Krause writes, "When creating a newsletter, a designer must find a balance between a piece that informs and a piece that the intended viewer will find exciting, entertaining, and/or interesting." The most important considerations for an effective newsletter are to be creative, concise, and consistent. Obviously, the publication needs to have visual appeal, flow well, and be user friendly, but if the writing is bad all that design effort was in vain.

Articles must be short and to the point. Freeman Tilden wrote, "Brevity is a critical component of good composition." Keeping articles short (200 words or fewer for news briefs) is easier said than done. Keeping writing short takes discipline. (Seventeenth-century French mathematician, physicist, and theologian Blaise Pascal once wrote, "I made this letter very long, because I did not have the leisure to make it shorter.") But that discipline pays off. The less space that is filled with text, the more space you have available to use for white space or for attractive images that assist with the communication of your mission.

Newsletters can be produced in a traditional print format or in an electronic format. Each format has common elements, but there are significant differences to consider during production. For electronic newsletters (HTML or e-mail), brevity becomes even more important. Readers typically take a few seconds to decide whether to delete an e-mail. The nature of electronic newsletters is that they must be quick, easy to read, and straight to the point. The best way to meet the goals of your electronic newsletter is to offer short blurbs with links to websites with additional information for those who want to find out more.

Consistency is the final important element of a good newsletter. Readers need to become accustomed to the newsletter's layout and where to find certain types of information. Regardless of format, a recognizable banner should lead the way, including logos, a title, and the date of issue. Under this element, referred to as the "flag" (not the "masthead"—as it is often mistakenly called), the next element that should follow is the lead story. Don't save the lead story for the inside, since many readers only read the front and back. In print, this layout can be in columns (an odd number is better), but avoid columns for digital versions. A reader may not completely read an article if he or she must scroll down and then scroll back up and then down again to read the remaining part of the article. A table of contents is a great element to add to the first page of a print newsletter or the top of a digital

■ Newsletters like *Eye on Nature* from Texas Parks and Wildlife Department help keep members and visitors informed.

The Making of a Logo

In November 2007, after more than a year of discussion and drafts, NAI unveiled a new logo. Perhaps more than any design element you will deal with, logos inspire passion and require attention to detail. Logos are the identity of your organization.

The description at right details the decisions that were made in developing the NAI logo. Once the concept was agreed upon (no simple task in itself), everything from the angle and thickness of the curved slash to the width of specific letters was up for debate.

Remember, too, that if you are replacing a logo that has been in use for 20 years (as was the case with NAI), you will surely encounter individuals who have developed an attachment to the old logo and resist the change.

■ NAI's previous logo served the organization well for almost two decades.

NATIONAL ASSOCIATION FOR
INTERPRETATION

This logo uses the unique interaction of the letters N, A, and I to create a form that is open to interpretation. The purely geometric right angles and straight lines convey professionalism and sophistication, while the organic, curved slash and exaggerated dot of the letter I speak to the friendly, informal nature of the field.

In addition, the typographic form creates the opportunity for viewers to add meaning. The form references potential readings in an abstract way, with the black portion representing the structured, built environment and the organic, colored elements represent the natural environment. The peaks of the letters N and A could be mountains or rooftops. The cross of the letter A could be the horizon or a river. The letter I could be read as a simple illustration of a human form or its dot could be the setting sun.

newsletter. This puts the reader in control and allows them to make decisions about investing time in reading this newsletter. A short, bulleted list can improve the overall use and success of a document. For digital formats, create the table of contents with hyper links to the story or item of interest.

Images and photographs are a great way to recognize volunteers, places, and events in a newsletter. In the print version make sure that the image is high-resolution and high-quality, prepared in such a way that the printing process (or photocopying) won't destroy the clarity of the image. In the digital format, you must consider download speed when considering which images and photos to use. High-resolution photos, too many photos, and photos that are too large can increase download time and will most likely cause the reader to close the program or stop the download. (See Chapter 5 for more on technical specifications of images for print or digital reproduction.)

Logos

The creation of an effective logo requires effort and painstaking attention to detail. A logo tells the world who your organization is or what it does, but it doesn't have to say everything all at once. Just as an interpreter should not try to overload an audience with information in a single presentation, a logo should not try to say all that there is to say about an organization. It is the face of your organization, not the whole body.

One important constraint in creating a logo is that it should be easily reproducible in a variety of media in different sizes. It needs to be consistent, but flexible enough to be reproduced in print (in one or multiple colors), online, embroidered, silk-screened, on a banner, on a billboard, or on a business card. If your logo will be used primarily in one medium or at one size—whether it be on a website or embroidered on a uniform—design it with that use in mind. Once you have decided how your logo will be used, the next step can begin.

In *Management of Interpretive Sites*, Tim Merriman and Lisa Brochu suggest that managers encourage staff "to have a creative brainstorming session that will result in developing meaningful memorabilia for interpretive experiences at your site." The same could be said for getting staff input on your logo. What is unique about your company? What is successful about your organization or message? What are others doing in your field and how do you compare to them? What is the image you want to portray? Answering these questions will help inform the design process, but should not necessarily dictate specific images that must be incorporated into the logo.

The reason those well-known symbols of corporations, from IBM to Coca-Cola to FedEx, are easily recognized is that they are simple. Simplicity of design must carry over into color palettes, typefaces, and graphics. One of the most widely known logos in the world is the Nike swoosh. It is simple, plain, clean, and symbolic. Keep logos such as the swoosh in mind when developing your logo. It should be noted, too, that the swoosh was not designed by a huge advertising firm. It was created in 1971 by a student named Carolyn Davidson, and Nike founder Phil Knight did not initially like the design but accepted it because he was up against a deadline.

Since you are creating something that you hope will be around for a long time, colors are essential in logo design. Be aware that some colors are trendy and that this year's hot color can be dated quickly. Harvest gold and avocado green are good examples of once-trendy colors that are now out of style. A host of professional sports teams came into existence in the 1990s, and it seems that nearly every one of them adopted teal, purple, and silver as its team colors. The consensus among sports fans now is that most of those teams look as though they are playing football, baseball, or basketball in their pajamas. Look at between two and four colors for your logo, depending on how it will be reproduced.

Exhibits, Wayside Exhibits, and Signs

In their book *Signs, Trails, and Wayside Exhibits,* Michael Gross, Ron Zimmerman, and Jim Buchholz state that "well-planned trails and exhibits can assist visitors in their search for connections to their heritage." Exhibits come in many varieties and terminology varies according to agency. The most common terms are wayside exhibits, temporary (interior or exterior), and large-scale permanent (interior or exterior). Signs are usually considered to be two-dimensional, but when they incorporate audio components, tactile components, or interactive components they become wayside exhibits. For any exhibit or sign to be effective, it must be read. To be read, it must be both visually attractive and well written. In *Environmental Interpretation*, Sam Ham writes, "Attractive exhibits are artistically pleasant and balanced, relying on interesting objects, visuals, and appropriate colors; they call attention to themselves."

Because they represent a substantial investment, most exhibits and signs will be professionally produced by a design/ fabrication contractor with input from site staff. The information that follows is intended to assist interpreters who will be part of that process but should not be considered a complete treatise on exhibit or sign design.

■ **Sandblasted/Routed Wood**

Advantages

- can often be produced in-house
- can be attractive if painted and well-maintained

Disadvantages

- maintenance required
- cost widely variable depending on imagery
- can be burned, shot, and otherwise vandalized easily

■ **Plastic Laminates/ Phenolic Resin Products**

Advantages

- full, vivid color
- durable in all situations
- gunshot holes easily repaired
- relatively inexpensive
- can easily be cut to custom shapes
- vandal resistant

Disadvantages

- production of plastic not always environmentally friendly

Advantages and Disadvantages of Common Sign Materials

LISA BROCHU

■ Metal/Aluminum

Advantages

- mid-range cost
- easily maintained

Disadvantages

- can be scratched easily
- gets extremely hot in direct sunlight
- limits use of color

LISA BROCHU

LISA BROCHU

■ Fiberglass Embedment

Advantages

- relatively inexpensive
- accepts digital prints

Disadvantages

- tends to crack and fade in extreme temperatures
- scratches easily
- shatters when gunshot

■ Porcelainized enamel

Advantages

- full, vivid color
- durable in extreme weather conditions

Disadvantages

- cost—long-term investment not feasible for changing messages
- rusts when porcelain surface is damaged

Today's exhibit and sign fabricators have techniques and skills that can create just about anything you can imagine—just be ready to pay for it. Research the materials that might be used and request samples from the contractor. Test the materials in a variety of environmental conditions and potential vandalism scenarios so that you have a sense of what your best options might be. Also try to find a another site that uses the same materials that is three to five years old and has the same environmental conditions as your location. This comparison allows you to see how durable the product is over time. Learn as much as you can about what you are buying and ask for a warranty to ensure that the product will be replaced if it does not stand up to the manufacturer's claims.

Even if you are contracting the design and production of exhibits and signs, you will likely have input on the development of the text. A short, clear, and concise theme statement should be your guiding light through the production. After your visitors have interacted with your exhibits or signs, the theme should be apparent to them. A good interpretive plan will keep exhibits and signs organized and thematic so that visitors have a complete, quality experience with little or no confusion about your purpose or the information you provide. The exhibit or sign title should convey the message but invite additional investigation of the exhibit or sign text, images, and other components. Subtitles help the reader decide how to invest their time by focusing their interest. Paragraphs of body copy (below the subtitles) must be concise. A good rule of thumb is between 50 and 75 words per paragraph, with no more than three paragraphs per sign or exhibit panel. Using the design principles already discussed in Chapters 3 and 4, think about placement of the paragraphs as separate items rather than one large text block. Three short paragraphs attractively placed are more likely to be read than one long column of text.

Think about how interior exhibits will work once they are installed. You will need maintenance access to change or clean elements from time to time, especially if live animals are involved. Make sure access is easy for dusting, cleaning, routine maintenance, and changing light bulbs. If your design includes high-tech gadgets and gizmos, ask for training from the exhibit production firm on how to fix common problems. If you are creating in-house exhibits, don't forget to provide an operations manual that details maintenance requirements and troubleshooting advice for staff who may come after you.

Think about safety and security issues as you design your exhibit. You may be surprised by what visitors, particularly children, will do in spite of warnings or the dictates of common sense. A good exhibit design and fabrication firm will pay atten-

PAUL CAPUTO

■ Once an exhibit or sign is installed, proper maintenance is essential.

tion to these issues during the design process, but you may have more experience watching visitors interact with exhibits, so don't hesitate to let your contractor know your thoughts. You also want to protect the investment in the exhibits themselves, as well as any items or artifacts you have on display. (For detailed information on sign materials, design, and applications, we recommend *Signs, Trails, and Wayside Exhibits* by Michael Gross, Ron Zimmerman, and Jim Buchholz.)

To ensure that the exhibit production firm you are using is following accessibility guidelines, become familiar with these standards yourself. The Americans with Disabilities Act (ADA) does not require that all exhibits be accessible. However, it does require that access to similar experiences must be provided to all. Because these standards change periodically, it's a good idea to check with the National Center on Accessibility (www.ncaonline. org) or the federal government's ADA website (www.ada.gov) to study the latest requirements. You might also consider testing your design ideas with individuals who are visually or mobility impaired to determine how accessible your exhibits really are.

The goal of exterior exhibits, waysides, and signs is to complement the visitor's experience, not to become a visual or physical obstacle. The design should complement the existing landscape and become a part of the experience through the use of native materials or materials that help convey the theme of the site.

Wayside exhibits offer the opportunity to develop multi-sensory experiences. Audio units can be added, but be cautious about overusing sound elements outside, where most people would prefer to hear the natural ambient sound. An expressive quote being read or the call of a bird on the exhibit can add an unexpected and interesting element. Also, raised relief or multiple layers can be added to incorporate the sense of touch. Whenever you add audio, tactile, or interactive components to outdoor exhibits or signs, be sure to consider the need for weatherproofing, especially in areas of high humidity or temperature extremes. Avoid the temptation to use bronze casts or metal signs in desert environments where they can become dangerously hot in direct sunlight.

Brochures

For a brochure to be an effective interpretive product, it must be valuable to visitors. What makes your brochure valuable and unique, especially if it is placed in a hotel or tourist center rack among dozens of others? In many cases only the top third of the cover can be seen in the rack. With that small space in mind you have to capture the visitor's interest, send your message, and

■ This exhibit at Parkin Archeological State Park in Arkansas features an audio component, which users control with buttons.

- Of the traditional folds for brochures, the single fold is the simplest, with one fold dividing a sheet in half.

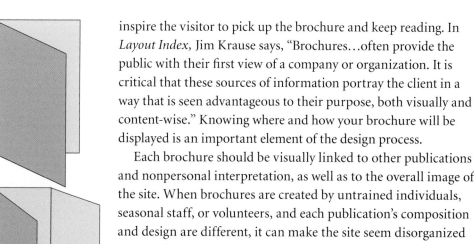

- The tri-fold brochure is extremely common. It is folded twice (in spite of its name) to create three panels.

- Gate fold brochures have four panels, with the outside panels opening like a swinging gate.

- Accordion fold brochures can have any number of panels. They collapse and open like an accordion.

inspire the visitor to pick up the brochure and keep reading. In *Layout Index*, Jim Krause says, "Brochures…often provide the public with their first view of a company or organization. It is critical that these sources of information portray the client in a way that is seen advantageous to their purpose, both visually and content-wise." Knowing where and how your brochure will be displayed is an important element of the design process.

Each brochure should be visually linked to other publications and nonpersonal interpretation, as well as to the overall image of the site. When brochures are created by untrained individuals, seasonal staff, or volunteers, and each publication's composition and design are different, it can make the site seem disorganized and confused about its own identity. The preferred approach is to use consistent typefaces, logo placement, and an overall style that expresses the underlying central theme for the site.

Brochures come in all shapes and sizes with multiple fold patterns. Typical styles include the gatefold (four panels that open up like a gate), tri-fold (which features three panels but is actually folded only twice), and the accordion fold (which can contain any number of panels and is folded in a zig-zag to create an accordion shape). Oversized and map-style brochures can have a strong visual impact, but often become too cumbersome to use and make it difficult to maintain flow through the document. Think about how the piece will be used before settling on a size. Will the large format double as a classroom poster? Will a driver on an auto tour have a problem seeing out the windshield when the map is unfolded? Test a few sizes and folds to ensure that you have the most effective solution to your need.

Once the size of paper is selected, the next step is to choose the paper itself. Paper quality is always an important design decision, but particularly so in the production of brochures, which are frequently subjected to folding, refolding, being stuffed in backpacks, or used as a picnic placemat. Durability is an important consideration, particularly if you have a high repeat visitation and expect visitors to use the same brochure more than once or return them for others to use. There is some evidence that a more attractive brochure on quality paper will have a higher perceived value and may even be kept as a souvenir item instead of being left on the trail as litter. Cheap, thin paper is rarely a good investment. In brochure racks, this paper will wilt over the edge of the rack, creating an unsavory image for your organization.

Flyers and Flats

Flyers and flats (single sheets with printing on one side) are used to promote programs, special events, resale items, and many other interpretive topics. A flyer, as defined by Jim Krause in *Layout Index*, is "a single-sided, letter-size, printed piece." Many interpreters are afraid to take on the creation of a brochure, website, logo, sign, exhibit, or multimedia program, but feel right at home with the development of a flyer or flat. But since poor design choices can limit the effect a flyer has on its readers, it is every bit as important to pay attention to these seemingly simple media choices.

Flyers and flats must grab attention through the use of text, space, graphics, and a concentrated message or information. Flyers do not allow much room for text, since they are small and the typeface point size has to be large enough to be read quickly from a distance. Titles should generally be kept to 10 or fewer words in nothing smaller than 16-point type and should convey the essence of the message. Details of who, what, when, and where can then be added as appropriate.

Placement of the headings and body copy are as important as what they are saying. Remember how people read. When looking at a flyer, the eye tends to center on the document first, then flows to the upper left-hand corner, and then proceeds to the right side of the page. This is where the decision of whether to continue takes place. If the reader decides to continue, the eye will drop down and to the left and continue reading the next line or interpreting the next image or element. If they decide not to read any further, the eye drops to the lower left-hand corner, scanning in-between, to make sure that nothing is missed. This common behavior is why your primary message (title) should appear in the top, left-hand corner of the flyer. Any other key information that you don't want users to miss (such as the website where they should register for the program) should be located in the lower, left-hand corner.

You need as much available white space (what designers call "negative space" or "counterform") as possible on flyers. If your flyer looks like a page out of the phone book from a distance, it will be quickly passed over. You have a limited space in which to maximize your message and must therefore concentrate the efforts of the reader into the small amount of text on your flyer. The more space, the easier it is to read, and the more likely it is that it will be read.

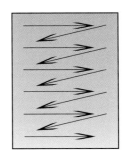

■ Eye-tracking research shows that in cultures where people read from left to right, their eyes move in a zig-zagging Z pattern starting at the top and moving down a printed page.

Websites

The Internet has changed the way visitors get information about interpretive sites. The potential for disseminating information to the public continues to expand at an amazing rate. Most interpretive sites can be found online through a simple Internet search, and this technology is used for everything from providing contact, calendar, and location information to providing guided, interactive tours as downloadable podcasts.

In *Interpretation for the 21st Century*, Larry Beck and Ted Cable write that "through technology, local nature centers and the smallest museums have expanded their sphere of influence both on-site and in the world beyond." Now that the World Wide Web has been around for many years, people of all ages and backgrounds are accessing information more than ever before. Today's visitors are making decisions about where they will go and what they will do based on a few minutes on the Internet, so your Web presence is directly related to your visitation and the potential for a positive visitor experience.

Nothing can destroy a potential visit like an out-of-date website. If you place information on the Web, then you should commit to keeping it current. Updates provided on a consistent basis will guarantee return visits to the site, which gives you the potential to get messages out over and over again. Your website should focus on what is special or unique about your interpretive center. This information should be visible on screen as soon as your front page loads.

Simple navigation is essential. Some of the most beautifully designed, artistic pages on the Internet are attractive but difficult to navigate. If a visitor to a site has to spend more than a minute getting oriented, they will be gone to something else or someone else's page. A listing of links and descriptions of adjoining pages should be available for simple navigation. Wherever the menu bar is placed, it should be placed in the exact same location on all adjoining pages. Contact information should be easily accessible. Have phone numbers, general information, email address, and physical addresses at the bottom of each page or located in an easy to find contacts link.

Avoid overloading the site with Flash or other plug-ins. Websites should be designed with the lowest common denominator in mind, technologically speaking. If you use advanced technology like Flash animation or other multimedia, be sure that visitors who can't access the feature see text, an image, or instructions on how to get the technology they are lacking. Remember that many visitors are in a demographic range that has been dubbed "digital immigrants"— those people who did not grow up with computers and are uncomfortable with any technology with which they are not familiar. These people are likely to bypass important information rather than seek out plug-ins or other downloadable features they don't understand.

The color palette of your site can also cause a user to leave prematurely. In many print projects, the colors at your disposal are limited. On the Web the color possibilities are nearly endless. The tradition online is to use a light background and a dark typeface, but as with PowerPoint or other on-screen media, stay away from pure black and white. Be sure that the background has some color or that your text is not pure black. Avoid long expanses of reversed-out type (white or a light color on a dark background), which can also be hard to read.

Take the time to view pages you design through different browsers (like Internet Explorer, Mozilla Firefox, or Safari), dif-

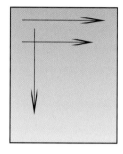

■ Recent research by the Neilsen Norman Group suggests that readers on the Web follow a rough F pattern, with two horizontal sweeps across the top of the screen, then a movement downward.

ferent operating systems (PC or Mac), different-sized monitors, and with different connection speeds. You may be surprised how different some things can look, and you may become aware of changes that should be made. Web design can be frustrating to the designer who insists on consistency, because the same page can look very different on different computers.

Maps

Visitors to your site need and want maps. Whether they use them appropriately, effectively, or at all depends on how well you create them. In *Interpreting for Park Visitors*, William Lewis writes, "When orienting visitors, it's important for them to know where they are, which way north is…especially if the instructions are the least bit complicated…remember what is perfectly clear to you is often confusing for another."

As defined by *Webster's Dictionary*, a map is "a representation of all or part of the Earth's surface." As you know, our Earth's surface is a complicated place. It is filled with roads, structures, signs, geographic features, bodies of water, people, and wildlife. Megan Kealy, in *Information Design*, says, "Maps reduce and rationalize our complicated surroundings to a simple representation." What may seem commonplace to us, since we live and work in these locations every day, can be very complicated to visitors. Our visitors are distracted; they are looking at views, checking out exhibits, keeping up with the kids, looking for the restrooms, or perhaps they are not accustomed to using maps. Maps need to be easy to read regardless of who is using them. If the map is not portable (mounted to a sign on the grounds or wall in the visitor center), be sure to orient the map to reality rather than north. Many people who have difficulty reading maps need the advantage of seeing the map oriented to the real lay of the land. If you fail to provide this common courtesy, expect to be looking for lost people and answering questions about directions even as you stand directly in front of the map.

Kealy also says:

You need to keep an open mind when drawing your maps and to draw reality as accurately as possible, so that first-time visitors to your park get the benefit of your longtime personal knowledge of the park. But watch out for your biases. Don't leave off information such as one-way roads because you know there are road signs telling visitors which way to go. Visitors never quickly grasp the layout of a complex developed area, such as the Yosemite Valley, just because you made a nice pretty map as though the place was uncomplicated. People will

■ Maps, either handheld or much larger, like this one at Governor Mike Huckabee Delta Rivers Nature Center in Pine Bluff, Arkansas, are essential to a positive visitor experience.

move comfortably through your park only when the map they hold in their mind and the map they hold in their hands agree.

How is your map to be used? What is the purpose of the map? Who is the primary audience? Secondary? How will the map be oriented? What will be the printed size of the map? How will the page be oriented? What is the map's scale? With so many questions to answer, it is no surprise that many maps are oversimplified. This oversimplification can work to your advantage in some cases, but more often it leaves visitors confused and leaves staff answering more and more questions.

Keep confusion to a minimum by making good design choices. Use one clean and simple sans-serif font. On maps, type should be supportive of the overall design, not a key element. Bold, italic, underlined, and decorative typefaces should be avoided. To emphasize text, the best option is to increase point size, but limit the number of point sizes to three sizes: one for major points of interest, including titles, key locations, obvious landmarks, and emergency locations; one for secondary points, including key roads, major intersections, landmarks, and important locations; and one for tertiary points, including secondary roads, trails, and other locations and markers.

Books

In either paperback or hardback, books are among the best keepsakes you can offer as a permanent memento of a visit to your site. They are an excellent gift shop item that allow you to provide collections of photography and interpretive writing for visitors who want to read in depth about your site's resources and possibly even share with others. Books with attractive photos and high-quality writing give visitors the chance to show off the photos they wish they had taken and say the things they can't quite articulate. If you don't have the budget to pay professional writers or photographers, photos and essays can be acquired through contests or collected from staff.

■ Opposite page: The elevated train in Chicago.

Avoiding a Train Wreck

One of the worst train disasters in history occurred near Salerno, Italy. On March 2, 1944, a long 8,017-passenger train with an engine on each end entered the Galleria delle Amri tunnel in the Apennine Mountains. One account states that when the engine on the front of the train stalled, the engineer at the rear of the train started up his engine to back the train out of the tunnel. Around the same time, the front engineer managed to get his engine started again and continued the journey forwards. Neither engineer had any way of communicating with the other. Both engineers thought they simply needed more power and should proceed as planned. They continued to pull in both directions for several minutes. Because of this miscommunication, over 500 passengers on the train died of carbon monoxide poisoning because two people were trying to go in different directions at the same time, leaving the train stalled in the tunnel.

Some projects can feel like a train with an engine on each end, pulling in different directions. This usually occurs when there is

Making the Collaborative Process Work

no specific person in charge of completing the project. Design is usually a collaborative process, but each person on the team must understand his or her role to reach a successful conclusion to the project.

As a designer, you may be the responsible party for transforming what is delivered to you into a format that is visually appealing, appropriately designed for the site, and easily used by visitors. Your work on the project may be just beginning as others' work is ending. Because you may or may not have been involved in the first part of the project, you may have to recognize that others who previously worked on the project have specific ideas about how it should be designed. On the other hand, you could be given *carte blanche* with very little direction and total freedom until time for final approvals.

As the creator or project manager, you may have personal interest in what you have created and timelessly researched, and you may have specific ideas about what the end product should look like. You know exactly why this project is being created and how it will affect your visitors or the bottom line of your budget. You may have been working on this project from its inception and find that, in the end, you are glad to get the project off of your desk and move on to something new. Your supervisor or manager may be asking you questions about when the project will be complete and why the project is overdue and beyond the budget. At some point in the process you may grow tired of working on the project and just be ready to see it done.

As the supervisor, you may be weighing considerations such as cost, time, and personalities. You have been monitoring the project throughout various stages but are unaware of specific details of how the project has developed or transformed.

You are concerned about how the team is working together. You are interested in seeing that the project is completed to the highest level and wonder how it will be received by your board of directors.

Whether your role is designer, creator, or supervisor, it is likely you'll have personal feelings and ideas invested in the project. Because of this personal interest, conflict may ensue. Conflict can be over tangible issues such as paper color or layout. Or it may be more intangible, resulting from simple personality conflicts between individuals. If there is conflict, being open-minded and prepared can turn a negative situation into one that yields positive results and solutions. For this to happen, all of the involved parties must be willing to be open to suggestions and must agree to be fair and objective.

If constructive disagreement turns to negative conflict, step back from the discussion and return to it later with a specific question to be answered or mission to be accomplished. Negative conflict is best conquered by collaboration. Through mutual efforts, expectations of all involved parties can be exceeded when the process works to its highest potential. All efforts could be lost if evasion, rivalry, or complacency rear their ugly heads during the conflict resolution. These elements of personality and conflict often occur naturally during the creative process, but by applying appropriate techniques, implementing specific procedures throughout the process, and keeping open lines of communication, the project will progress, and it won't be long before you can see the light at the end of the tunnel.

Dealing with Designers

For nondesigners working with professional designers, there is often the perception that designers are fragile artists and in fact, some of them seem to be anxious to encourage that perception. But being viewed as artists often oversimplifies the role of the graphic designer in your project. First of all, designers are not necessarily artists. Many designers have artistic qualities and appreciate a certain visual aesthetic, but the primary function of graphic design is to organize information and solve problems. Most designers do not view their work as art, but rather as a synthesis of information. As problem solvers, designers employ a system to impart data in a format that is accessible, eye-catching, and user-friendly.

Most designers have a process that they go through when creating. These processes can vary greatly from designer to designer. Most designers are accustomed to dealing with deadlines and alterations late in the process. They know how to work under stressful conditions. Making your expectations clear, understanding your designer's expectations, and fostering a solid working relationship with your designer will help you develop a better product.

Pitfalls of Collaboration

Be aware of barriers that could impede good communication. If you bring assumptions, attitude, bias, partiality, preconceived notions, or unwarranted emotions, communication could be interrupted. Each person involved should know his or her role in the creative process. Some may see the designer as the person responsible for the assembly of what was created by the interpreters; others may include the designer in the early steps of the creative process, even as early as inception, to incorporate their ideas in the early phases. If you know there is potential for conflict, include the designer in the entire process.

Designers are responsible for establishing the visual identity of a product, so if they are not given all of the information as to what the identity of the product should be, they have to come up with it on their own. This may work well sometimes, but often it creates miscommunication. Since many interpretive sites already have a well-developed identity, be sure that the designer you are working with understands the vision and mission of your site. Remember that designers can give information character by providing this identity and shaping the overall aesthetics of a product. When collaborating with designers, be sure to take the lead and communicate with them about what you expect, want, and need from the design process.

Take time early in the project to meet with all of the involved parties (limiting it to key stakeholders), develop a plan or agenda, and follow through with it. Keep minutes or notes of who is responsible for which elements; share those notes after the meeting or at the end of the meeting. Make sure that all of those who are involved know what their responsibility is at the time the meeting is adjourned.

■ Good communication is essential to a successful project.

Finding and Working with an Outside Designer

The *Brand Identity Guidelines* from the National Parks Conservation Association (NPCA) has this to say about selecting a graphic designer:

> Desktop publishing has opened up a whole new universe for all of us, but just because it is possible to do, does not mean it is a good idea. And everyone who describes himself or herself as a designer is not necessarily good at it. So before you choose a designer for your project, be sure to get examples of his or her work. Do they have experience with the sort of project you have in mind? Have they designed advertisements, policy papers, brochures, or special features for a magazine before? Have they worked with NPCA before?
>
> Also be sure to get a bid on your project, and be clear about expectations. Does the bid include a lot of back and forth for changes and revisions? Does it include preparing the document for a printer? Does the designer plan to work directly with a printer or are you expected to handle that end of things? Revisions can add up quickly, and usually a designer will include some leeway in the bid for this, but very few tolerate five or six rounds of revisions without charging extra.

If you are contracting with an outside designer or design firm, your first step should be to define exactly what services you need. It is a waste of your time and the designer's time to request bids if you don't know what role you want the designer to play or what the difference is between various types of designers. Do you need a graphic designer or an exhibit designer? Will your designer be involved with developing a theme or initial concept? Or will he or she be expected to lay out and design text and images that have already been developed and approved? Take the time to review your site's mission, goals, objectives, and any pertinent plans prior to deciding on a project. Once the approach is approved, put some effort into defining the project: what it is now, what it will be, how much it should cost, how much you have to spend, what the deadline is, who will be involved, the goals it will accomplish, and the need it meets.

Write a list of specifications with as much detail as possible. If you are entering the process with a designer from the very beginning or the concept phase, the statements could be very vague but directed towards the goal, objective, or mission (something like "The contracted designer or firm will be responsible for creating a complete concept for a website that meets the first interpretive goal of the park's interpretive plan."). If you are involving the designer only in the latter stages after the content has been approved, the scope of service can be more specific (for instance, "The contracted designer or firm will lay out the provided edited text into a brochure format and prepare print-ready electronic files in QuarkXPress to deliver to the printer.").

Through the creative process, various groups and individuals bring something of benefit to the table. Designers have the potential to contribute to this process if they are needed and if they are capable. It is possible for designers to have agendas, be stuck in ruts, and not be inclined (or qualified) to play certain roles in the process. Meet with potential designers early on and establish their level of comfort or expertise with your subject matter, and work within their base of knowledge. Make sure the guidelines and

■ Define the services you want performed before contacting a freelance designer.

expectations are clear, free of jargon, and outline what you want the end product to be. Once the project is laid out through the written specifications, your energies can be focused on selecting the best designer available.

If you know someone who has worked with a designer on a project similar to yours, be sure to ask that person for a recommendation. Even if you don't know someone, you can seek them out. If you run a nature center, contact similar organizations and find out with whom they work. If they are happy with the work of a contracted designer, ask their permission to contact him or her yourself. Even if the designer has a full schedule, he or she may be able to make a recommendation. You can also find designers of interpretive projects in NAI's *Interpreter's Green Pages* (www.interpnet.com).

When selecting a designer, it's important to know what sort of characteristics and abilities you're looking for. Graphic designers don't necessarily design the components of interactive exhibits and vice versa. An exhibit designer may have a background in graphic design, but perhaps more importantly, he or she should understand industrial design to be able to create three-dimensional working components of exhibitry. A cabinetmaker is not necessarily an exhibit designer. All of these individual skill sets may be needed to develop quality exhibits, so you should take care to identify the right skill set for your project before attempting to find the right designer or design team.

Once you know what you're looking for, you can begin to narrow down your choices. The first cut may be simple, based on matching the skills of the designer to the requirements of the job. The second cut may be more difficult, as some individuals will have overlapping skill sets. It's a cliché

to say "Trust your gut feeling" or "You'll know the one when you see it," but it can be true. If you have ever made a decision to do something and your instinct was telling you to do something else, perhaps you can relate. If you are questioning a designer's ability or skill, there may be something wrong. If you are wondering if this person can follow through with anything in a timely manner, you may be on to something from instinct. This feeling is often related to personality and may not be directly related to the type of work the person does. It is related directly to how well you may work with this contractor. Use experience as your guide. If you have little or no experience in hiring a designer, find someone who does and have that person accompany you to the interview to provide you with their input.

Designers and design firms will have portfolios for you to peruse in person, online, or both. If they don't offer one, ask to see some of the work that they have done for clients similar to you or your organization. While looking through their body of work, begin by looking for a type of product that they produced that is of the same genre of what you are looking to have produced. If you are planning to use this person or firm to design a website, you will want to see other sites that they have created. If you're looking for interactive or live-animal exhibits, make sure they have experience in designing those elements. Don't rely on the "If they can do that, they can surely do this" principle. Just because they have design skills and training, all of their experience could be in creating digital products and not what you need for another type of project. They may have the ability to design the piece but no experience working with printers or exhibit fabrication firms. Don't be afraid to ask specific questions about their work. Ask questions like:

- What specifically did you do on this brochure/exhibit/sign?

- What is the weight of this paper?

- What were printing costs on items such as these?

- What sort of reactions do visitors have to this exhibit?

- How can you make our product stand out from these?

These questions will help you develop an understanding of their knowledge as well as confirm their involvement.

Interviewing Designers

An interview of the proposed contractor should always take place. The effort applied to the front end of hiring a designer can save you countless hours of work, money, and frustration on the back end. During an interview the conversation is often about the product or project at hand, when the focus should be on the designer and his or her capabilities, experience, and success. If you have your concept developed, it can be okay to share what you are looking for. Just focus on the designer and how he or she can help you reach the goals of the project. Pay attention to how much research the designer or firm has put into learning about your area of interest. If they have put effort into learning about you or your site, then they may be conscientious and willing to work for you. If they have made little or no effort to learn about you or your site, then that should be a warning.

As with most other types of job interviews, you should look for professional behavior like timeliness, appearance, and other qualities that may be important to you or your site. If you feel the interview has gone well and that you have found a potential contractor, towards the end of the interview, provide them with a set of specifications about your project and what you expect the designer to bid on. Within these specifications you can outline the project, your stated goals, and deadlines for completion. Based on the written specifications that you provide, the designer should be able to provide you with an hourly rate or an overall quote bid for his or her services as well as an estimate of production costs.

As with any person or firm that you would be contracting with, ask for a list of references. If they are hesitant or unwilling, that could also be a warning sign. Any decent designer will be willing to provide you with a list of satisfied clients. Be sure to contact the references provided. It is often assumed that if the contractor provides you with a list of references then the references are going to say good things. This is not always the case. Some may be just hoping you don't call and check. The references very well may say good things, but you should listen for what they don't say as well as what they do. Ask about work habits, ability to meet deadlines, personality types, strengths, weaknesses, communication issues, budget issues, or anything that could have happened during their production process with the designer. Some references may be reluctant or unable to say anything negative due to their agency's policies. If you sense that is the case, ask whether or not they would hire the designer again. Your overall goal is to find out if others have been satisfied with their work and how you may be able to create a satisfactory work relationship with them. By attempting to find out how successful they have been at working for clients, you will have some assurance that they will see your product to fruition.

The majority of designers cannot stand

alone in their successes. Knowing this, take the time to inquire as to who their partners in success are. **Working with partners** can be a science in itself. Much of how a designer will work with partners can be discovered through the interview. As previously discussed, you will develop a gut feeling about how well you can work with this person and that same feeling can be applied to how they would be expected to work with partners. A designer may be perfectly competent in his or her abilities to design, organize, and create, but if he or she lacks the skills to work with printers, photographers, writers, editors, illustrators, interpreters, managers, and even technical support personnel, then success can be lost. If a designer has worked successfully with a printer or supply house, then this partnership can save your project many hours trying to find a potential sub-contractor. Partners can also serve as problem solvers. If the designer has a great relationship with a partner, then ideas, problems, and other issues can be presented to them for solutions. It's not always about what the designer knows, but whom he or she knows, that gets the project done.

Interpersonal skills of the designer can be of utmost importance. If a designer does not have the ability to relate to you, your site, or the project, he or she probably lacks the needed proficiency to complete the project successfully. Interpersonal skills include the behaviors and conduct that are used around others as well as finely developed skills in listening, diplomacy, and etiquette used in communication. Many interpersonal relationship skills are developed early in life and are either evident or not. To some degree, these skills can be taught or learned, but often they are inherent. If a person has some element of the skills, he or she can be

coached to improve this ability to communicate but you may not want to take the time to coach them on how to work with a team. You want to work with designers who have well-developed interpersonal skills because once they are a part of your team, their actions reflect on you or your site. Designers with strong interpersonal skills will be able to control emotion in difficult situations in order to see that the project stays within parameters and will thereby increase efficiency of the team. Increased productivity is what you hope for through effective communication.

Be sure to consider both verbal and nonverbal interpersonal skills. Some clues to their ability to communicate will be how they send (speak) and receive (listen to) messages during the interview. If they don't make eye contact, are positioned away from you, seem distracted, are not focused, don't repeat elements of the questions that you ask, or ask questions themselves, then their interpersonal skills may not be well developed. Look for those designers who speak to you in your language, respond suitably to questions, use open-ended questions, project legitimate interest in their voice, have appropriate facial expressions and confident posture, and seem amenable. If you are debating between two possible designers with similar skills and abilities, choose the one with highly developed interpersonal skills for your project.

The Educated Designer
Education in design is something that should not be discounted in the selection process. How much education or what type of education a designer should have before being considered a designer often sparks debate within the profession. There are many people working in the field of graphic design who have little or no

Dealing with Nondesigning Designers

On occasion, you may find a non-designing designer. By this, we mean individuals who possess some technical expertise, training, or experience, but who are not formally trained in the tenets of graphic design. They have just enough knowledge and skill to get them in trouble.

Within interpretive sites, there is often an employee who has been deemed the designer (possibly against his or her will). This task is usually given to this person because he or she possesses computer skills or artistic talents. Again, just because a person is artistic doesn't make that person a good designer. As interpreters, we are often thrust into design by default. This could be because of the typically outgoing personalities of interpreters, the many and varied duties that come along with the job, or the creative requirements of the position. At times, this unwitting interpreter/designer is simply the person who has always done it all along.

If you find that you are a non-designing designer, invest time in the earliest stages of development, clearly defining what is wanted out of the project: how it will be used, what sort of look and feel it should have, and what information should be included. Try to learn as much as possible about design—not just how to use certain technology, but the principles of graphic design. This book is a good start, but you should read further about the type of design specific to your responsibilities (some suggestions for additional reading can be found in the resources section of Chapter 8 of this book). If time and budget constraints allow, take a class online or at your local college or university. Design is a life-long learning process; the more you delve into it, the more you will recognize how it provides the basis for everything around us, whether it is nature's design or human-made.

formal education or training. They may have trained under a designer, developed personal skills, be artistic and computer savvy, or just have an intuitive design ability. A designer with "street knowledge" of design may be perfectly able to complete your project to your level of satisfaction, but he or she typically cannot provide the same level of skill and expertise of an educated designer. An educated designer will bring more to the process and be able to make more well-informed decisions about concepts, layout, color, space, and other elements of design. Good designers also need to possess technical skills in working with current software, hardware, and techniques.

A minimum of an associates degree is required within most design firms for entry-level positions. Coursework for an associates degree can include elements of typography, color, illustration, composition, photography, software, and hardware to develop a base knowledge of basic design elements. A bachelors degree is required of most designers working for a firm as junior graphic designers. Depending on the school the graphic designer attended, their coursework will include elements of writing, psychology, sociology, cultures, marketing, business, art history, creativity, printing techniques, designing for the Internet, commercial graphics, and electronic imaging. For exhibit designers, coursework in industrial design, electronics, and mechanics is also part of the mix.

A graduate education is increasingly common in the field of design. A graduate degree, typically a master of fine arts (which, like a Ph.D., is a terminal degree), often provides the designer advanced skill or specialized ability within the disciplines of design. At this education level, the designer should not only possess a full working knowledge of the technical aspects of project design, production, and completion, but also bring conceptual ideas to the process. Designers today are being called upon for more than just layout and are now being included in the earliest development phases in order to participate and contribute to the writing, editing, and other parts of the creative process. A designer with a bachelors degree, at a minimum, or preferably, a master of fine arts, can meet the advanced needs of organizations and interpretive sites.

What to Provide to the Designer

Once you have selected a designer, be sure to ask how he or she would like the materials delivered. Most designers will want text and images as separate files. Don't try to do the designer's work for him or her, because that usually leads to extra work for your designer. Text should be unformatted; every chart, inserted text box, or attempt at some sort of visual layout is work that your designer will have to undo before formatting it in page-layout software. Indicate in the text approximately where images should be placed, but do not import them into your word processing file. Images should be provided in their original format, either as digital images direct from your camera or as hard copies. Every attempt you make at cropping, retouching, or scanning will interfere with your designer's ability to work with that image.

The National Park Service Solution

The National Park Service (NPS) realized that in many of its park units, there were nondesigning designers who were responsible for creating brochures, site bulletins, flyers, maps, and websites for their particular site. With so many creating original documents across the near 400 NPS units, a consistent style or identity was difficult to achieve. The NPS Graphic Identity Program was created to be a mission-driven way of unifying the delivery of information so that messages could be presented consistently and effectively. The program traces the history of NPS and how identifiable elements such as the uniform, campaign hat, and the arrowhead logo were created, designed, and adopted as a standard.

The program details such elements as the appropriate use of the NPS arrowhead logo (full-color versus black-and-white versions of the logo, which logo to use at certain sizes, the implications of print compared to Web applications, etc.). The manual covers basic design elements such as typography and the composition of signage and wayfinding products. The NPS has two approved fonts for use on documents as part of its graphic program. The font NPS Rawlinson was specifically created for NPS as a traditional, easy-to-read serif font. Frutiger is a classic sans-serif font (developed in 1968 by Adrian Frutiger for use on signage at Paris's Charles de Gaulle Airport) adopted by NPS as its typeface for titles and applications where legibility is essential.

Through the program, a set of templates was created for download from the Web to be used by NPS personnel. Important design standards used for communicating the image of NPS were incorporated into the templates. The templates allow for individual or site freedom within the framework, while still establishing a clean, consistent, recognizable identity. Most importantly the Graphic Identity Program was developed by professional designers and founded on sound graphic design principles. Overall, the program defines a consistent identity for NPS products without telling the interpreter what should be included or how the message should be crafted.

Dealing With Nondesigning Editors and Supervisors

If you are a designer (or you are not a designer, but you have been thrust into that role), you have a supervisor. It may be a direct supervisor or a paying client. Either way, in most cases the designer must answer to someone. The person who oversees the designer may have little or no design training or understanding. This could be a positive, as the supervisor or client may acknowledge the expertise of the designer and trust his or her judgment. However, it could make it difficult for the designer, having to work within the construct of someone else's preconceptions about what a project should look like or how it should function. As the designer in this scenario, you should make sure that your role in the process is clearly understood by you and your supervisor. More importantly, you should be prepared to defend your decisions and educate your collaborative team about the meanings behind the decisions you have made.

Presenting more than one idea at the beginning of the process will allow the rest of the creative team to respond to what they like about each one. If you are working on a new website, develop multiple concepts (usually a minimum of three) and present mock-ups to your client or supervisor before investing everything in one concept that may be rejected. Once you have developed a strong working relationship and an understanding of what your supervisor or client responds to, this may become an unnecessary step, but at the beginning of a relationship, it's an important step. Don't present the client with an idea that you do not like just to have an additional option. Murphy's Law dictates that the one you don't like will be the one that is accepted.

If you have a unique concept that you envision as a strong solution to a problem, allow time for your supervisor or client to react. Asking for an on-the-spot reaction to a concept that is outside the realm of expectations will most likely result in a negative reaction. Give your client or supervisor several days to get used to an idea. This will help them become accustomed to what is being created and will allow time for them to buy into the concept.

Also, be thick skinned and open to comments. Nothing inhibits the collaborative creative process more than a supervisor who sees the designer as an artist who is fragile and takes his or her work too personally. Alternatively, it is not healthy for the process if the designer sees his supervisor as ignorant of the genius of his or her concept. A designer may love an idea, but if it is not well-received even after an attempt or two at defending it, it's time to move on.

If there is not a site publication plan or even a simple set of design guidelines, work to get one created. This can be a large

■ Presenting multiple concepts at the beginning of a project, as with these postcards from City of Rocks National Reserve in Idaho, is a good way to get the conversation rolling.

publication (like the one used by the National Park Service) that identifies everything from the amount of white space that needs to appear around a logo and the exact line spacing that needs to be used with each typographic point size, or it can be a single sheet of paper that identifies preferred fonts and colors. In the case of design disputes, this type of document should be the first place you look for a solution.

The most effective way of dealing with non-designing supervisors is by developing the right mind-set. If you know what you have done is effective and high quality, get your mind set to take the issue and educate your supervisor about the reasoning behind your design decisions. Be prepared to give and take. Often, success involves some level of compromise; in other instances compromise may not be an option. When you find middle ground, run with it. If difficulty persists, take a step back and look at similar products generated by your site or agency or a similar site or agency. Bring in an outside, impartial opinion, someone who has not necessarily been involved in the process to this point. Most importantly, work together to find solutions.

When to Break the Rules

Use that third typeface! Place that photo off the grid! Pick a color that has nothing to do with the palette of the rest of the project!

It has been said that rules are made to be broken. This is true in the world of graphic design, though stepping outside the box is easier for some than others. For those personality types that are more rigid, it can be difficult to even consider changes in approach. There is a certain amount of safety in rules, and with safety comes comfort that many designers use as a crutch. Rules about color usage, page composition, and typography are there for a reason, and they help the designer create

legible, organized, meaningful communication. But the negative side of rules is that they can limit the way we think about solving design problems.

When the rules fail, they should be broken. A broken rule will create emphasis, as readers will notice an oddly cropped photo or a font or color that they haven't seen before. Once you know the rules and how to implement them, the freedom to break them should be used to your advantage.

Designers should be aware that there may be extra effort or even danger (that's right—*danger*) involved when breaking the rules. The overall success of a product could be affected by one broken rule. If an author begins breaking too many rules when writing, then the reader may become bemused or the intended message can be lost, muddled, or ignored. But used in the right way, a broken grammatical guideline can add emphasis or attention to a specific point. Many authors unapologetically use sentence fragments to drive home a point. Sentence fragments! Just remember that while there are consequences to rule breaking, if the designer can defend the meaning behind the decision in a meaningful way, then it is legitimate. Breaking rules can be empowering, leaving the designer with a personal connection to a project that creates a level of commitment that is often impossible otherwise to create.

There is a culture that revolves around risk, and within any culture there are positives and negatives. There are many rule breakers out there today who veer from the norm not only on occasion, but as much as possible, and have achieved great success. Pop artist Andy Warhol and Apple Inc.'s Steve Jobs are examples of designers (of one sort or another) who broke rules. Postmodern philosopher Jacques Derrida

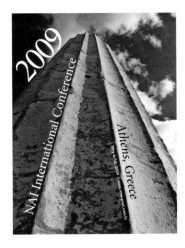

■ The cover of the registration packet for NAI's 2009 International Conference in Greece breaks the rules. For maximum legibility, type should not be set on an angle. However, here, the type follows angles defined by the architectural column, contributing to an overall effect that draws the viewer's eye upward.

and architect Peter Eisenman published a book titled *Chora L Works* with meaningfully placed holes drilled through the final printed product, making some text impossible to read. This was met with consternation, to say the very least (reader reviews of the book on Amazon.com give an idea of how the concept was received). Renowned graphic designer David Carson pushed the limits of legibility in *Ray Gun* magazine and other products, obscuring type, using abstract fonts, and manipulating images nearly beyond recognition.

Generally, it's more about how the designer or the agency employing the designer deals with risk. Some risk is predictable—good or bad—and not as difficult to take into consideration. Value is a second consideration: Is the risk worth it, and is it timely or cost effective?

The most important element to remember when breaking a specific design rule is to know the rule you are breaking and why you are breaking it. It is not enough to understand that you are violating a basic design standard by centering all of your text. You have to know why you are doing so and what value it brings to the product.

If you break a rule to add emphasis, you want to really break it. If you add a color from outside the palette you have established for a project, the new color should not be too close to the other colors you've used, or it will simply look like a mistake rather than a purposeful design decision.

If the breakage is purposeful, then it can be justified and effective, and it can add to the intended emphasis that you are searching for in the design. For example, if you have established a strong grid throughout a document and you need to add extra emphasis to a title or photo, stepping outside the grid may be the best way to draw attention to it. When the dust has settled, you should always reevaluate to see if the deviation was successful and if it achieved what you wanted it to.

Project Evaluation

Evaluation can be an important management tool. It can be used to encourage future projects, illustrate the importance of interpretation, direct policy, and even attract funding. Evaluation in the design process is one of the most important steps, and it is too often left by the wayside. Often a project is completed and a product is in use but it is never re-evaluated—even before reprinting or publishing.

So, why evaluate? The project is already complete. The majority of the effort was put into the design phase. The project meets the intended needs—or does it? Evaluation will let you know for sure. One of the reasons it's important to have a list of intended goals for a project at the beginning of the process is so that you have a set of criteria by which to evaluate the project once it is implemented. If you don't begin planning for the evaluation process until after the product is in use, you will never really know its true effect.

Evaluation should assess the overall effectiveness of a product. While one must look at what the original intent of the product was and focus on the goals and objectives that were established early in the process, the unintended outcomes that a product may produce, both positive and negative, are equally important. Review the goals and objectives established at multiple stages through the project to measure success. The objectives that were created should have been measurable, making it feasible to quantify results. These may include invested time, financial impact, visitor results, and allocation/utilization of resources, to mention a few.

Other less tangible criteria for measuring success may be established as well. These criteria can include effects on team dynamics, overall management, adjusting to changing conditions, or meeting unplanned needs of a project. While tangibles are easier to measure, measuring intangibles requires a specific effort that often produces results that are open to interpretation.

How the evaluation is conducted is important. Time and effort should be placed in how the sample will be taken and in what manner. Who is conducting the evaluation is also of importance. The evaluation can take place from an in-house committee or an outsourced firm. There are pros and cons to either option. While an in-house group may develop a strong sense of ownership of the project, they may be too close to the project to truly be objective. Of course, they maybe the cheaper alternative. If an outside firm is used, they may be goal oriented, better at meeting deadlines, and objective, but they require more effort on the front end. Explaining the project and its intended outcomes and goals can be costly.

Success is often somewhat subjective and difficult to determine. As interpreters, it is not uncommon to have delusions of grandeur. Our projects have meaning and purpose, and like our children, we want them to succeed. As with anything in life, sometimes we are disappointed with the outcome. More often than not, the information provided from evaluation does not produce "saving the world" statistics. Ideally you would rank a project as successful if it were completed under or within the budget, within the established timeline, with strong bottom-line results, a happy staff, some positive effect on the resource, or positive changes in visitor behavior.

Why Projects Fail

Some of the most common reasons projects fail are universal. Knowing elements that have led to other failures, either at your site or at similar sites, can help keep your project from failing. The most common aspects of failure come from time, budget, planning, and personalities involved.

If you don't have realistic goals for completing a project within a specific time frame, time and money will be lost. A realistic budget should be created in the early phases of the creation process, adhered to, and adjusted as needed to meet the goals of the entire project. If you know that being over budget is a threat, monitor expenses closely. Being on time is directly related to money and the budget. If you don't have a realistic timetable with realistic deadlines, money will be wasted. Without deadlines, projects can go on for years with changes of scope, change orders, and never-ending edits, all costing your site money in design fees and hours of labor, not to mention mental stress on your staff. Projects that drag on and on open themselves to complete loss of scope or changes in intent. When loss of project mission happens, it can lead to additional elements that weren't intended, planned, or budgeted. When a project has been ongoing for long periods of time with no end in sight, stop the process and reevaluate what is taking place and focus on the original goals. Adopt a realistic time scale with deadlines and stick with it; it pays off in the end.

Not having the appropriate skill set represented on your team can play a role in failure. In the field of interpretation, diverse backgrounds are common. When beginning the creative process, involve the best individuals with education or experience that relate to the project. If you don't have the people with the skills necessary

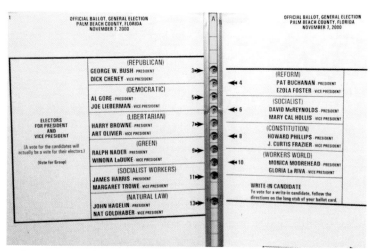

OFFICIAL BALLOT, GENERAL ELECTION
PALM BEACH COUNTY, FLORIDA
NOVEMBER 7, 2000

OFFICIAL BALLOT, GENERAL ELECTION
PALM BEACH COUNTY, FLORIDA
NOVEMBER 7, 2000

(REPUBLICAN)
GEORGE W. BUSH · PRESIDENT
DICK CHENEY · VICE PRESIDENT

(DEMOCRATIC)
AL GORE · PRESIDENT
JOE LIEBERMAN · VICE PRESIDENT

(LIBERTARIAN)
HARRY BROWNE · PRESIDENT
ART OLIVIER · VICE PRESIDENT

(GREEN)
RALPH NADER · PRESIDENT
WINONA LaDUKE · VICE PRESIDENT

(SOCIALIST WORKERS)
JAMES HARRIS · PRESIDENT
MARGARET TROWE · VICE PRESIDENT

(NATURAL LAW)
JOHN HAGELIN · PRESIDENT
NAT GOLDHABER · VICE PRESIDENT

ELECTORS
FOR PRESIDENT
AND
VICE PRESIDENT

(A vote for the candidates will
actually be a vote for their electors.)

(Vote for Group)

(REFORM)
PAT BUCHANAN · PRESIDENT
EZOLA FOSTER · VICE PRESIDENT

(SOCIALIST)
DAVID McREYNOLDS · PRESIDENT
MARY CAL HOLLIS · VICE PRESIDENT

(CONSTITUTION)
HOWARD PHILLIPS · PRESIDENT
J. CURTIS FRAZIER · VICE PRESIDENT

(WORKERS WORLD)
MONICA MOOREHEAD · PRESIDENT
GLORIA La RIVA · VICE PRESIDENT

WRITE-IN CANDIDATE
To vote for a write-in candidate, follow the
directions on the long stub of your ballot card.

■ Sometimes the reason a project
fails is simple: bad design, as with
Palm Beach County, Florida's infamous
butterfly ballot in the 2000 presidential
election. Note how the line above
"Democratic" leads straight to the
notch for Pat Buchanan.

to complete the project, it is destined to fail. Search to make sure that your team is balanced and effective. This is easier said than done, but it can be the difference between failure and success. If you are struggling to find the personality or skill set that you need to enhance the project, don't forget about possible partnerships with volunteer programs, teachers, professional associations, and universities that may all be willing to help.

If the people on your team have the appropriate skills, but they can't work together, it can lead to difficulties. Some people may have the needed skills to compete the project but they just don't work well together. The skill of working well with others can be as important as technical knowledge. If you have an unwanted dominant personality, he or she may have to be eliminated from the process or be given strict guidelines as to their approved level of participation. Again, this is easier said than done, especially if the person is a key stakeholder. The project manager should be empowered to deal with the situation and should have the skills to effectively communicate issues and lead the project.

Staff continuity is a major factor in maintaining good working relations. Many people in the workforce today are either retiring or moving on to the next best position. This has great impact on project completion, especially at interpretive sites with small staffs. This is where solid planning can lead to success. If a plan is created and laid out, regardless of who is running it, it can be completed. If the project is vague and misguided from the beginning, it will fail with or without staff changes.

When Things Don't Work Out

A failed project hurts. At some point in time a design or product we create is going to flop. As mentioned above, the products interpreters create are like our children, and when they don't succeed we take it personally. So, what can be done with a design failure? We live in a culture that is afraid of failure, and there are very few examples of how to deal with it or to bounce back from it. Failures can happen for a multitude of reasons, and it is often a combination of factors that lead to ultimate failure. Personal conflict, misunderstandings, tunnel vision, personal vendettas, unrealistic assessment of weaknesses, and a lack of leadership, funding, market knowledge, or original ideas can all be factors.

During the early stages of the creative process, take time to define a list of threats to the project. This is an opportunity for all of the involved parties to surface any ideas running through their conscience that may be telling them that the project is not going to happen. An anonymous approach may be an effective approach. Have involved parties drop thoughts about **threats to the project** in a box to be compiled and reviewed as a group later. The anonymous approach allows the process to be more honest, and a team member's insecurities about being perceived as negative or harsh can be circumvented. After the list has been approved, compiled, and edited, formulate approaches and options to effectively thwart the threats and transform them into challenges that can be met and overcome. Once the full team is aware of all of the possible threats team members can think of, they can be handled to the best of the team's abilities as they arise.

Evaluations give the creators of a project some idea of when a product is in trouble. Knowing this allows designers to prepare for failure. If there is an undercurrent that goals will not be achieved, this is when it is time to act. Don't allow it to happen, intervene with ideas or a brainstorming session, assemble the committee, circle the wagons—do your best to predict and circumvent a failure in the making. Don't be afraid to plan for failure in order to be ready to adapt.

If you fail, try again. Remember that your failed project—whether it was produced and did not meet its goals, or even if it never made it to production—can be a learning opportunity. Analyze what went wrong and how those mistakes can be avoided in the future. Many products that are used on a daily basis by millions of Americans came out of failure and second attempts. So, if Thomas Edison can fail, fall flat, and bounce back, then so can interpreters.

■ Opposite page:
African elephant
image found on
the free stock
photo website
Stock.Xchng.

A parable speaks of an ancient village in which all of the inhabitants are blind. While traveling from one town to the next, six of the blind men came upon a man riding an elephant. The men had heard of elephants, but never had the opportunity to get close to one, so they asked the rider if they could touch the animal to learn what an elephant was really like. Each of the six men approached the elephant and touched it until they felt confident about what an elephant looked like. Upon returning to their village, many of the other villagers gathered to hear about their great encounter with the elephant. The first man to speak said that an elephant is like a huge spear. He, of course, had only felt the tusk. The second man, who felt the side of the elephant, said that an elephant is more like a solid wall. The third to speak said that they were both wrong, for he had felt the elephant's ear, and an elephant was more like a leaf that was alive. The fourth, having touched the elephant's trunk, said that an elephant is more like a giant snake. The fifth, who touched the elephant's leg, said that the elephant was more like a moving tree, solid and strong. The

Resources

sixth man said that all of the others were wrong, and since he was given a ride on the elephant, he said that the animal was more like a moving mountain. Still, to this day, the men who met the elephant argue about what an elephant is really like.

Learning about design is like learning about the elephant in the parable. Each resource that you attempt to learn from, whether it is a book, website, class, person, or periodical, has a different perspective and can reveal only a portion of what there is to know. You can learn from any of the aforementioned sources and take details from each. Just remember that in order to gain a full understanding of what design is, you need to hear from all six men who touched the elephant and put all the pieces together. Most importantly, bring your own perspective to each of the resources listed here (and others that you find), synthesize the information that resonates with you, and begin to develop your own visual voice.

While there are many, many resources available to designers online and in print, those listed below are some that the authors have found useful.

Interpretation and Interpretive Planning

The National Association for Interpretation (NAI)
(www.interpnet.com)
NAI is a not-for-profit professional organization currently serving about 5,000 members in the United States, Canada, and over 30 other nations. Individual members include those who work at parks, museums, nature centers, zoos, botanical gardens, aquariums, commercial tour companies, and theme parks. Commercial and institutional members include those who provide services to the heritage interpretation industry. NAI's mission is to inspire leadership and excellence to advance heritage interpretation as a profession. This mission is accomplished through providing training workshops of regional, national, and international scope, a certification program, newsletters and periodicals, a peer-reviewed *Journal of Interpretation Research,* and a variety of other programs, products, and services.

Environmental Interpretation: A Practical Guide for People with Big Ideas and Small Budgets
by Sam H. Ham
One of the most popular books in the field, this book is written specifically for people with big ideas and small budgets. Drawing on 20 years of experience and the successes of his colleagues worldwide, Sam Ham presents low-cost, time-tested communication techniques. The book includes practical techniques rooted in a solid theoretical foundation. Readers learn not only how to communicate their ideas more forcefully but why the methods work.

■ Environmental Interpretation by Sam Ham

■ Interpretive Writing by Alan Leftridge

Interpreting Our Heritage
by Freeman Tilden
Now in its 50th anniversary edition, *Interpreting Our Heritage* has been a sourcebook for those who are responsible for interpretive materials. Whether the problem is to make a prehistoric site come to life or to explain the geological theory behind a particular rock formation, Freeman Tilden provides helpful principles to follow.

Interpretive Planning by Lisa Brochu
The 5-M Model outlined in this book is drawn from the author's 25 years of experience in creating interpretive plans, and explains the process she has taught to hundreds of interpreters. This book can be a valuable tool for those wishing to develop an interpretive plan as well as those aspiring to work as a consultant or planner.

Interpretive Writing by Alan Leftridge
This book introduces you to the strategies promoted by the National Association for Interpretation and the National Park Service for written interpretation, with a focus on developing tangibles, intangibles, universals, and interpretive themes in your writing, while avoiding trite expressions. These strategies and skills apply to your brochures, websites, exhibits, public service announcements, books, magazine articles, and other interpretive projects.

Interpretation for the 21st Century
by Larry Beck and Ted Cable
Building on the interpretive principles of Enos Mills and Freeman Tilden, *Interpretation for the 21st Century: Fifteen Guiding Principles for Interpreting Nature and Culture* presents a vision for effective interpretation into the next century. This book offers guidance and inspiration for anyone who wishes to learn more about interpreting our cultural and natural heritage.

Management of Interpretive Sites
by Tim Merriman and Lisa Brochu
This book will help you develop managerial and leadership skills. Whether you need to write personnel policies, develop a business plan, conduct meetings, or use interpretive efforts to convince visitors to become stewards of your resource, this book contains specific suggestions based upon the authors' combined 60 years of experience in running not-for-profit, governmental, and for-profit organizations. For interpreters working in the field of graphic design, this book will help you understand the role you play in the larger picture.

Personal Interpretation
by Tim Merriman and Lisa Brochu
Though this book is about personal rather than nonpersonal interpretation, it addresses basic tenets of interpretation that any interpretive designer should understand. It employs the most current ideas in the interpretive profession. It also shares some of the rich traditions from interpretation's past masters, drawing on Freeman Tilden's principles and Enos Mills's thoughtful ideas on nature guiding. It will connect you with the more in-depth resources developed by authors such as Sam Ham, Bill Lewis, Douglas Knudson, Ted Cable, Larry Beck, and Joseph Cornell.

■ Interpreting Our Heritage, 50th Anniversary Edition by Freeman Tilden

■ Personal Interpretation by Tim Merriman and Lisa Brochu

Design of Interpretive Materials

Signs, Trails, and Wayside Exhibits
by Michael Gross, Ron Zimmerman, and Jim Buchholz
This is the third volume in the Interpreter's Handbook Series. This is a useful book for anyone developing interpretive signs or wayside exhibits. It addresses valuable information about planning, development, crafting, and important concepts related to signs and wayside exhibits.

Designing Interpretive Signs: Principles in Practice
by Gianna Moscardo, Roy Ballantyne, and Karen Hughes
This comprehensive guide provides a series of principles for effective sign design, with instruction based on research, the latest in educational and psychological theory, real-world examples, and practical guidelines. The book includes valuable information about choosing sign locations, attracting and keeping visitors' attention, organizing information so that visitors can easily follow it, and generally improving signs for a wide range of sites.

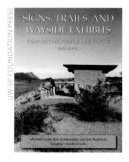

■ Signs, Trails, and Wayside Exhibits by Michael Gross, Ron Zimmerman, and Jim Buchholz

Graphic Design for Beginners

Graphic Design Cookbook
by Leonard Koren
This book exposes readers to stimulating ideas that can be applied to books, flyers, brochures, websites, and newsletters. The book offers various organizational palettes to assist with layout issues that will make your publications better.

Design for Communication
by Elizabeth Resnick
From basic to advanced, graphic design techniques covered in this book assist readers with developing a unique approach to design issues. With over 42 design assignments included, hands-on applications become your trainer.

The Non-Designer's Design Book
by Robin Williams
This book addresses basic design principles as well as an introduction to typography. It has a clear, simple approach to design that anyone can use and leave learning something new.

Robin Williams Design Workshop
by Robin Williams and John Tollett
This sequel to *The Non-Designer's Design Book* takes Williams's writing and techniques to the next level. More in-depth and challenging, this book opens up a dialogue of discussion about composition, visual impact, challenges, and inspiration.

Design It Yourself by Ellen Lupton
This book deals with everything from designing for T-shirts to creating logos. After reading it, you will think more like a designer and know how design processes can be applied to various formats. Its cutting-edge design as well as unique approaches will inspire you to create.

Typography and Composition

Elements of Typographic Style
by Robert Bringhurst

This comprehensive book about typography is essential, especially for those new to design. It offers historical context as well as discussion of how to choose and combine type, compose pages, and establish rhythm and proportion in a composition. Bringhurst uses principles from such fields as mathematics and music when discussing page composition.

Grid Systems in Graphic Design
by Josef Müller-Brockmann

This book is the standard bearer on using grid systems in graphic design. The text, written in 1961, is still useful today for anyone working in design. With examples of both simple and elaborate grids and discussion of how to work at a conceptual level, this book is, at its root, about problem solving.

Type in Motion and Type in Motion 2
by Matthew Woolman

Type in Motion was the first book to present an overview of animated typography and *Type in Motion 2* is its successor. These beautifully illustrated books present examples of animated type with descriptive captions, focusing on the role of type in delivering information, story-telling, interactivity, and experimental design.

Typographic Design: Form and Communication
by Rob Carter, Ben Day, and Philip B. Meggs

Now in its fourth edition, this book is relevant for those using electronic media or traditional print media. The book addresses topics such as how letters are constructed, type families, the aesthetics of visual communications and design, and legibility. One particularly enjoyable element in the book is timelines that demonstrate changes in the field of typography from a historical perspective, beginning more than 5,000 years ago with the first signs of written language to current-day Web and multimedia design.

■ Elements of Typographic Style by Robert Bringhurst

Inspiration and Discussion of Graphic Design

Print Magazine

Print describes itself as "a bimonthly magazine about visual culture and design." The magazine offers discussion of design in its many permutations. It is a general-interest magazine with a stated target audience of designers, art directors, illustrators, photographers, educators, students, and enthusiasts of popular culture.

Communication Arts Magazine

Communication Arts is a popular magazine with articles about graphic design, photography, and advertising. It highlights top work in the field of design and hosts competitions in advertising, multimedia, photography, illustration, and design.

Webmonkey (www.webmonkey.com)

Webmonkey.com is a forum for Web designers at all levels. It provides tutorials in design, construction, multimedia, e-commerce, and programming. The monkey bites blog keeps subscribers up to date on news and trends within the Web development and design communities.

Color

Interaction of Color by Josef Albers

One of the quintessential books written about understanding color, this was originally intended as a guide for artists, teachers, and students. It contains studies—some of them real mind-benders—of how colors work together. The author was a member of the modernist Bauhaus group in Germany in the 1920s.

■ Interaction of Color by Josef Albers

Logo Design

Big Book of Logos by David E. Carter and Logo Design edited by B. Martin Pedersen

These popular series present literally thousands of logos from around the world. If you're developing a logo or identity, these books are sources of inspiration and ideas.

Logo Lounge (www.logolounge.com)

This website is dedicated to the logo. News, trends, and factors affecting logos are discussed, and users can easily access a database of logos.

Green Production, Supplies, and Materials

Forest Stewardship Council (FSC) (www.fscus.org)

The FSC is a nonprofit organization that certifies printers, paper stocks, and many other related sources that use environmentally friendly practices. By promoting responsible behavior in every important step of the production process, from management of the forests that are harvested for paper to the disposal of waste at print shops, FSC certification is becoming increasingly important. Many designers require that printers be FSC certified and use FSC-certified paper before even soliciting a price quote.

Online Image Resources

Federal Agency Photos

Some federal agencies provide images for free download to the public. The National Park Service (http://photo.itc.nps.gov/storage/images), USDA Forest Service (www.fs.fed.us/photovideo), Bureau of Land Management (www.blm.gov/wo/st/en/bpd.3.html), and Library of Congress (www.loc.gov/rr/print/catalog.html) all have such sites. If you can't find what you want online, we recommend contacting specific sites directly. Site administrators are often happy to share photos or direct you to the appropriate party in exchange for nothing more than a photo credit.

Stock.Xchng (www.sxc.hu)

This website offers high-quality, peer-reviewed images to download for free. Like most such sites, it requires a free username and password. It is a member-driven community, so photographers (even amateurs) can upload their own images for consideration, chat with other members, and peruse tutorials and blogs by members. Stock.Xchng's sister site, Stockxpert (www.stockxpert.com), offers images for sale.

Note that the photo of the elephant at the beginning of this chapter was found on Stock.Xchng. Also, you can download high-resolution photos (including some found in this book) by Paul Caputo at www.sxc.hu/profile/pcaputo.

Flickr (www.flickr.com)

Flickr.com is an online image management application that allows designers to upload, organize, share, and find images. The basic free service and Flickr blog offer opportunities and assistance to keep designers from losing control of photos and image files.

iStockPhoto (www.istockphoto.com)

iStockPhoto.com is a member-driven community that provides access to photos, images, and graphics. As a member, you can buy or sell stock as well as find free images. The website is easy to use and is a great place for generating ideas.

Veer (www.veer.com)

This website offers photography, illustrations, and typefaces for sale. Many of their products are available free or through trial memberships. They also offer promotional items from time to time. In addition, an "Ideas" section of the site offers the opportunity to browse and seek inspiration.

■ This photo of Vancouver, Canada, is one of hundreds of thousands of stock photos available at Stock.Xchng.

Font Resources

Adobe Fonts (www.adobe.com/type)
Adobe is one of the industry leaders in font development and technology. Its online catalog offers high-quality postscript fonts for sale.

MyFonts (www.myfonts.com)
Billed as the complete online source for finding, trying, and buying fonts, the format of the webpage is easy to use and navigate, which makes this page a valuable resource.

Free Mac Fonts (www.freemacfonts.com)
Just as it sounds, this site is a resource for Mac users to download free fonts.

Trends, Market Information, Culture

The Experience Economy: Work is Theatre & Every Business a Stage
by B. Joseph Pine II and James H. Gilmore
This book details the state of what the authors call "The Experience Economy," an economy in which businesses (and interpretive sites) succeed not by merely offering services, but experiences. This is a valuable book for interpreters hoping to understand market trends.

Blink: The Power of Thinking Without Thinking
by Malcolm Gladwell
In this book, the author argues that split-second decisions are often more valid than considered ones, that too much information can corrupt the decision-making process. He explores the role of instinct and intuition in society.

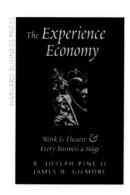

■ The Experience Economy by B. Joseph Pine II and James H. Gilmore

TrendWatching (www.trendwatching.com)
Trendwatching.com is an independent trend firm, dependent on a network of over 8,000 trend spotters that provide subscribers with access to information about trends and insight into global markets. A free subscription provides members with a monthly "Trend Briefing" filled with a new and interesting look at products and consumer tendencies. The firm also provides reports and keynote addresses. For designers the site stimulates the mind for new products, formats, services, and experiences.

Trend Hunter online magazine (www.trendhunter.com)
Trendhunter.com is an online community and database dedicated to being on the cutting edge for consumers and the curious. *Trend Hunter* helps generate ideas, stimulate creativity, and ultimately move designers ahead of the curve. *Trend Hunter* features micro-trends, viral news, and pop culture. The most popular micro-trends are later grouped into clusters of inspiration in a trend report, a tool for professional innovators and entrepreneurs.

Professional Associations

American Institute of Graphic Arts (AIGA) (www.aiga.org)

The mission of the nonprofit professional association AIGA is to advance designing as a professional craft, strategic tool, and vital cultural force. Founded in 1914, AIGA offers publications, online resources (including job listings and directories of designers), and discounts on training and conferences. AIGA focuses on the culture of design and current trends more than it does on specific technology or techniques.

National Association of Photoshop Professionals (NAPP) (www.photoshopuser.com)

NAPP (the Photoshop one, not to be confused with the National Association of Patent Practitioners) is a member organization that is about more than just Photoshop. It addresses issues of technology and design, and offers a number of benefits, including online training, publications, conferences, and networking.

Software Support

As inaccessible as some software may seem at times, the companies that produce design programs want you to know how to use them. Whatever software you use, there are multiple resources available for a variety of learning styles.

Built-in tutorials that come with the software walk you through the basics step by step. The help function that comes with the software allows you to seek solutions to specific problems.

Many software companies offer free online training, especially when they are unveiling new versions of software. Find the website for the software you want to learn about and get on their mailing list to learn about when these online tutorials take place.

It is often possible to find third-party trainers who offer classes for a fee. Again, an online search will reveal a bounty of these resources.

Books such as the "For Dummies" series and the "Quickstart Guide" series are inexpensive and comprehensive resources for getting started and eventually mastering software, available for most software at bookstores or online.

One Final Warning

Be advised that once you enter the world of design, you can never look at a brochure, website, menu, book, street sign, or any other venue where type and image interact the same way again. Look at this affliction as an opportunity for professional development and enjoy your new perspectives.

Happy designing!

Glossary

Adobe AfterEffects
A powerful computer program typically used by professionals for animating graphic elements in film or video.

Adobe Director
Computer program typically used by professionals for creating animations or interactive elements, frequently for stand-alone media like CD-ROMs or interactive kiosks.

Adobe Dreamweaver
Computer program used to design and build websites.

Adobe Flash
Computer program typically used by professionals for creating interactive elements, animations, or games for websites or video.

Adobe Illustrator
Computer program typically used by professionals for creating and manipulating vector-based images.

Adobe InDesign
Computer program typically used by professionals for publication design.

Adobe Photoshop
Computer program typically used by professionals for correcting and retouching photographs, manipulating existing images, or creating original digital art.

Adobe Photoshop Elements
A less expensive, less powerful version of Adobe Photoshop.

Analogous Colors
Any two or three adjacent colors on a 12-part color wheel. These create low contrast when used together.

Arm
Horizontal stroke of a typographic character with at least one end that does not connect to another stroke, like the top stroke of a capital T.

Ascender
Stroke of a typographic character that extends above the mean line.

Ascent Line
Imaginary line that indicates the point to which ascenders of typographic characters extend in a font. Sometimes extends beyond the cap line.

Banner
A leading graphic on a newsletter that contains title information, logos, and publication information.

Base Line
Imaginary line that indicates the lowest part of a typographic character that does not have descenders.

Bowl
Rounded stroke of a typographic character.

Brainstorming
Group or individual process where ideas are shared without criticism to solve a problem.

Brochure
A publication, normally involving multiple folds, that can be used to present various interpretive messages.

Cap Line
Indicates the point to which the top of capital letters in a given font reach.

Centered Typographic Alignment
Text set so that each line is centered symmetrically on an axis.

Central Theme
The main message or big idea that provides guidance for all interpretation products at a site.

Collaboration
A process where a group works together to solve a problem creatively.

Concept
An idea, where a large amount of time and effort have not been invested, presented in a clear, understandable format used to gain permission to proceed.

Conflict
A struggle between incompatible personalities, concepts, or ideas that leads to lack of production.

Contrast
The degree to which visual elements in a composition are juxtaposed to one another.

CorelDRAW
Computer program typically used by professionals for creating and manipulating vector-based images.

Counter
Enclosed portion of a letterform.

Counterform
See "White Space."

Cerebral Hemispheres
Description by Roger W. Sperry of the sides of the brain responsible for different types of thinking (artistic on the right, logical on the left).

Clip Art
Generic, cartoonish images often placed in compositions by amateur designers. (Not to be confused with illustrations.)

CMYK Color Mode
Stands for cyan, magenta, yellow, and black, and refers to the pigments used to create colors in printed materials.

Color Palette
Specific colors designated for use as part of an identity system for a series of compositions or within a single composition.

Color Wheel
Devised by Isaac Newton, explains the relationship colors have to one another.

Columns
Vertical guidelines in a composition that define the arrangement of text and images.

Complementary Colors
Colors that oppose each other on the color wheel, like blue and orange, and create high-frequency color palettes. Note that the term "complementary" derives from "complete" (as in, these colors complete the color wheel), rather than the more common understanding that they "compliment" each other (or look good together). Lots of colors compliment each other. Only complementary colors oppose each other on the color wheel.

Continuous-tone Images
See "Pixel-based Images."

Cool Colors
Green, blue, and purple are associated with cold temperatures partly because they evoke water and ice.

Creative Process
From initial concept to final production, a series of steps that an individual or group endures to solve a problem or complete a task.

Creative Writing
Descriptive prose or poetry that expresses an idea using allegory, metaphor, or other verbal devices.

Decorative Typeface
A set of highly expressive and ornamented typographic characters. Should be used sparingly, if at all.

Depth of Field
Effect of having the focal point of a photograph appear in sharp focus while the foreground and/or background are out of focus. Usually achieved by adjusting the aperture on a single-lens reflex camera.

Descender
Stroke of a typographic character that extends below the base line.

Descent Line
Imaginary line that indicates the point to which descenders of typographic characters extend.

Digital Immigrants
People from a generation outside that of the information boom, who did not grow up with any technology.

Em-dash
Typographic character, a dash the width of the letter M (—), used where you might otherwise use a colon or parentheses.

En-dash
Typographic character, a dash the width of the letter N (–), used to indicate duration, as in "The birdwatching program is scheduled for 11:00 a.m.–2:00 p.m."

EPS (Encapsulated Post Script)
File format typically used for vector-based images.

Exhibit Designer
An individual with a background in preparing conceptual, schematic, and construction-level drawings of three-dimensional exhibits.

Feedback
Input provided to a designer throughout the creative process. Feedback should be solicited from those close to a project as well as those with no emotional attachment.

Flush Left/Ragged Right Typographic Alignment
Text set so that the left side of a column aligns while the right side does not. Commonly used for body copy.

Flush Right/Ragged Left Typographic Alignment
Text set so that the right side of a column aligns while the left side does not. Should be used sparingly.

Flyer/Flat
A single-sided publication used primarily for promotional or advertisement purposes.

Focal Point
Portion of an image that draws the viewer's eye.

Font
A single typographic style within a typeface. For instance, Helvetica bold is a font within the Helvetica typeface.

Found Object
Physical item (as opposed to an image or other representation) that is incorporated into a composition.

GIF (Graphic Interchange Format)
File format, typically for use on the Internet, most appropriate for images with sharp edges and no blending between colors.

GNU Image Manipulation Program (GIMP)
Free computer program typically used for correcting and retouching photographs, manipulating existing images, or creating original digital art.

Graphic Artist
An individual who prepares or creates images to be used in the design of interpretive media.

Graphic Design
The practice of coordinating type and image in compositions in an organized, systematic, and visually appealing manner.

Graphic Designer
An individual who coordinates type and image in compositions in an organized, systematic, and visually appealing manner.

Grayscale
Refers to black-and-white images that include shades of gray.

Grid
Simple, useful system of organizing visual elements in a composition. Sometimes called the International Typographic Style.

Hierarchy
Differentiation between the importance of visual elements in a composition, usually divided into primary, secondary, and tertiary levels.

Horizontal Axes
Imaginary guidelines across a composition that guide the placement of elements on a page.

HTML Editor
A type of computer program used to design and build websites.

Hue
A color at full intensity, with no white or black diluting it.

Hyphen
Typographic character used for breaking words from one line to the next or combining compound words or phrases.

Illustration
High-end drawn image created by a professional (or talented amateur) artist.

Illustrator
An artist who creates images for use in exhibits, signs, or other interpretive media.

iMovie
Computer program for the Macintosh operating system used for downloading and editing video files.

International Typographic Style
A grid layout that uses vertical and horizontal axes to guide the placement of elements in a composition.

Interpersonal Skills
Inherent or learned techniques that a person has that improve communication and problem-solving skills.

Interpretation
A mission-based communication process that forges emotional and intellectual connections between the interests of the audience and the meanings inherent in the resource.

Interpretive Plan
Documentation of the planning process that blends management concerns with resource considerations and audience desires and ability to pay to select the most appropriate media to communicate a message.

Interpretive Writing
Writing that adheres to interpretive principles and connects readers both emotionally and intellectually to the resource.

Jargon
Specific or technical language of a profession, trade, or organization.

Journalism
Writing style that captures the facts of who, what, where, why, and when.

JPEG or JPG (Joint Photographic Experts Group)
File format that compresses continuous-tone images, typically for use on the Internet.

Justified Typographic Alignment
Text set so that both the left and right sides of a column align.

Kerning
A term used to describe the tightening of space between letters (sometimes used interchangeably with "letterspacing," though that is technically incorrect).

Keynote
Computer program for the Macintosh operating system used for making simple multimedia presentations using text, images, and sometimes video files.

Leading (pronounced like "Letting")
The measurement, usually in points, of the amount of space between lines of text. The term derives from strips of lead typesetters put between lines of type on a plate for a printing press.

Left Brain
The cerebral hemisphere associated with logic and organization.

Letterspacing
A term used to describe the widening of space between letters (sometimes used interchangeably with "kerning," though that is technically incorrect).

Logo
A symbol, which may or may not include text, that represents an organization, site, event, or specific idea, and that is easily recognized and understood.

Map
A two-dimensional representation of a three-dimensional environment.

Margin
Imaginary guidelines at the edges of a composition that guide the placement of the outermost portions of that composition.

Mean Line
Imaginary line that indicates the top of a lower-case typographic character with no ascender.

Media
Anything that communicates a thematic message to an audience. May include, but is not limited to, exhibits, signs, publications, programs, websites, broadcasts, food service, playground equipment, sales items, and promotional materials.

Message Element
A theme, subtheme, or storyline for specific media that supports the overall central theme for the site.

Microsoft Expression Web (formerly Microsoft FrontPage)
Computer program used to design and build websites.

Microsoft PowerPoint
Computer program used for making simple multimedia presentations using text, images, and sometimes video files.

Microsoft Publisher
Computer program typically used for publication design, usually for projects to be printed in-house rather than with a professional printer.

Monochromatic Colors
Color scheme based on a single hue (or color) from the color wheel, creating contrast and variation through tints (adding white) and shades (adding black).

Monospaced Font
Set of typographic characters that each take the same amount of horizontal space, as would be seen on a typewriter.

Multisensory Experience
Involving all of the senses (sight, sound, touch, smell, and sight) into the interpretive experience, whether personal or nonpersonal interpretation.

Neutral Colors
Gray and brown, made by mixing complementary colors.

Newsletter
Presented in hard copy or digital format, used to communicate an organization's mission and update a specific audience of news events.

Nonpersonal Interpretation
Sometimes referred to as passive interpretation, does not require a person to deliver the message to the audience once it is produced (e.g., exhibits or signs).

Objective
A specific, measurable statement that provides guidance for planning, used as an evaluation tool.

Orphan
The awkward placement of a single syllable of a hyphenated word on a line by itself at the end of a paragraph.

Pantone Matching System (PMS)
International standard for creating thousands of specific colors, usually for printed materials.

PDF (Portable Document Format)
File format that lets designers prepare layout proofs or final printable documents without requiring others to have specific software or fonts on their computers.

Personal Interpretation
Sometimes referred to as active interpretation, requires a person to deliver the message to the audience (e.g., campfire programs).

Pixel-based Images
Photographs, fine art, or other digital images made up of a finite number of pixels, also called "continuous-tone" images.

Plug-in
Optional software application that adds functionality to pre-existing software.

Primary Colors
Red, yellow, and blue are the only pigments that cannot be created by combining other colors.

Production Schedule
Organizational system that assigns dates for the completion of specific tasks throughout the creative process.

QuarkXPress
Computer program typically used by professionals for publication design.

Resolution
Concentration of printed dots or on-screen pixels in a continuous tone image.

Reversed-out Type
White or light-colored type on a dark background.

RGB Color Mode
Stands for red, green, and blue, and refers to the light frequencies that create images on screens and monitors.

Right Brain
The cerebral hemisphere associated with artistic and creative thinking.

Rule of Thirds
Well-known rule of composition that advises that images or compositions be divided into three equal parts horizontally and vertically, with important visual elements falling on those guideline.

Sans Serif
From the French *sans* for without, describes a typographic character whose strokes terminate without ornamentation.

Saturation
The purity of a color (a color at 100 percent saturation contains no white or black).

Secondary Colors
Orange, purple, and green are created by combining two primary colors.

Serif
Flared end of a stroke on a typographic character.

Shade
A color made darker by adding black to it.

Site Publications Plan/Graphic Design Standards Manual
A set of graphic design standards established to maintain a consistent message, purpose, and direction across various media.

Signature
Set of 16 bound pages in a publication that results from one large sheet of paper folded and cut to size.

SLR (Single-lens Reflex) Camera
A high-end camera with changeable lenses and manual controls of settings like shutter speed and aperture.

Specifications
A set of specific statements or characteristics that outline the desired output for a contractor to deliver.

Stem
Primary stroke of a letterform.

Stock Photography
Collection of royalty-free photographs offered for a fee or for free, depending on the source.

Technical Writing
A direct, descriptive style of writing that provides specific instructions.

Template
A file with pre-established design elements to limit the amount of design decisions that have to be made in creating various applications. Usually associated with various types of software.

Tertiary Colors
Colors created by combining primary and secondary colors on the color wheel.

Theme
A succinct central message about a topic of interest that a communicator wants to get across to an audience.

TIFF (Targeted Image File Format)
File format typically used for images in printed or manufactured compositions.

Tint
A color made lighter by adding white to it.

Typeface
A family of fonts. For instance, Helvetica, Helvetica bold, Helvetica italics, and Helvetica bold italics are four distinct fonts, all part of one typeface.

Typography
The art and science of laying out typographic characters in a composition.

Vector-based Images
Digital images composed of mathematical formulas or paths. These contain sharp edges or computer-generated gradients (a blend from one color to another color).

Visual Identity
A recognizable collection of applications, including a logo, website, or other products that represent an interpretive site's mission, normally defined through a set of guidelines.

Warm Colors
Yellow, orange, and red are associated with warmth in part because they evoke things like sunlight and fire.

Wayside Exhibit
An exterior exhibit that interprets the significance of the site or area where it is placed. They are often used as way-finding or to explain decision opportunities for visitors.

Website
Internet-based resource managed by a site, agency, or organization.

White Space
Area of a composition intentionally left free of design elements, helps keep the composition clean and guide the user's eye to important information.

Widow
The awkward placement of a single word or very short line of text at the end of a paragraph.

Windows Movie Maker
Computer program for the Windows operating system used for downloading and editing video files.

X-Height
Measurement from base line to mean line of typographic characters. Can vary from font to font (making some fonts look larger than others, even at the same point size).

INDEX

Acrobat Reader, 60
active/personal interpretation, 3, 6, 113
Adobe AfterEffects, 61, 107
Adobe Director, 61, 107
Adobe Dreamweaver, 60, 107
Adobe Fireworks, 57
Adobe Flash, 60, 61, 78, 107
Adobe Fonts, 104
Adobe Illustrator, 57, *57*, 59, 60, 107
Adobe InDesign, 59, 60, 107
Adobe Photoshop, 43, 56, 59, *59*, 60, 107
Adobe Photoshop Elements, 56, 60, 107
Adventures of a Nature Guide (Mills), 5
aesthetics, 21
Albers, Josef, 102
Albuquerque, 26, 36, *36*
Aldus Pagemaker, 59
American Institute of Graphic Arts (AIGA),
    105
Americans with Disabilities Act, 75
analogous colors, 27, *27*, 107
apostrophes, 35
Arizona Sonora Desert Museum, *14*
arm, 34, *34,* 107
ascender, 34, *34,* 107
ascent line, 34, *34,* 108
audience/audiences:
    defining by function of project, 8
    interpretation principles and, 4
    knowing and understanding, 8, *8,* 9, *9*
    matching readability of materials, 15–16
    matrix of audience characteristics, 8, *8*
    monitoring trends/market information,
        104, *104*
    reading patterns of, 46, 50, 77, *77*
    selecting target market, 8, *8,* 9
audio programs, 15, 71, 75, *75*

Ballantyne, Roy, 100
banner, 108
base line, 34, *34,* 108
Beck, Larry, 5, 78, 99
Big Book of Logos (Carter), 102
bleeds, 47
*Blink: The Power of Thinking Without
    Thinking* (Gladwell), 104
Bonnell, Mary Ann, *44*
books, as permanent mementos, 80
Boulder County Parks and Open Space
    Department:
    Agricultural Heritage Center, 12, *12*
    Stroh/Dickens Barn Exhibits, 12, *12*
bowl, 34, *34,* 108
brainstorming, 21, 108
Brand Identity Guidelines (NPCA), 84
Brecon Beacon National Park, *16*
Bringhurst, Robert, 101
British Columbia, 36, *37, 38*
Brochu, Lisa:
    on creating logos, 71
    on interpretive planning, 5, 7, 99
    on interpretive principles, 2
    role in NAI certification and training
        programs, 1

brochures:
    capturing interest in, 75–76, *76*
    consistency and overall style, 76
    as first contact, 5
    folded options, 76, *76*
    identifying audiences with, 9
    interpretive messages in, ix, 108
    paper quality, 76
Buchholz, Jim, 46, 71, 75, 100, *100*

Cable, Ted, 5, 78, 99
campfire programs, as personal
        interpretation, 3
cap line, 34, *34,* 108
Caputo, Paul, 1, 2, 103
Carson, David, 30, 92
Carter, David, 102
Carter, Rob, 101
centered typographic alignment, 35, 108
central themes, *10,* 11, *11,* 12, *12,* 108
cerebral hemispheres, 21, 108
Chesapeake Bay Maritime Museum, *3*
Chicago, elevated train in, *81*
City of Rocks National Reserve, *90*
clip art, alternatives to, 43, *43,* 44, 108
CMYK color mode, 55, *55,* 56, 108
collaborative process:
    avoiding train wrecks, 81–82
    breaking the rules with purpose, 91–92
    dealing with non-designing designers, 88
    defining threats to projects, 95
    factors/causes of project failures, 93–94,
        94, 95
    finding and hiring professional designers,
        83, 84–89
    good communication/preventing barriers
        to, 83
    managing personalities and conflicts, 82,
        108
    planning for evaluation, 92–93, 95
    presenting multiple concepts, 90, *90,* 91
    roles/responsibilities of team members,
        23, 82
    specifications/design guidelines for
        designers, 84, 89, 113
    working with nondesigning editors and
        supervisors, 90–91
color/colors:
    affecting overall message, 6
    analogous, 27, *27,* 107
    CMYK color mode, 55, *55,* 56, 108
    complementary, 27, *27,* 108
    on computer monitors, 55, *55*
    cool colors, 28, *28*
    creating contrast, 46–47, *47*
    as cultural or historical resource, 26
    as design element, 25, *25,* 26, *26*
    hue, 28, 110
    intensity/saturation, 28, 113
    monochromatic, 27, *27,* 112
    neutral colors, 28, 112
    Pantone Matching System (PMS), 55, 112
    primary colors, 26, *26,* 113
    on printed materials, 55, *55*
    reason for using, 26
    resources and inspiration, 102, *102*
    RGB color mode, 55, *55,* 57, 113
    secondary colors, 26, *26,* 113

shade, 28, 113
tertiary colors, *26, 27,* 114
tint, 28, 114
vocabulary of, 28, *28*
warm colors, 28, *28,* 114
color palette, 78, 108
color wheel, 26, *26, 27, 27,* 109
Communication Arts, 102
complementary colors, 27, *27,* 108
composition:
    balancing with white space, 47–48, *48,* 114
    bleeding elements, 47
    creating contrast, 46–47, *47,* 48, *48*
    hierarchy of text and images, 45–46, *46,*
        47, *47,* 48, *48,* 77, *77,* 110
    organizing/aligning with grid layouts,
        48–51, *51*
    primary/attention-grabbing, 45
    secondary/supporting text and images,
        46, *46*
    tertiary elements, 46
computers:
    file formats for print purposes, 56, *56,*
        57, *57*
    files for screen or projected media, 57–58,
        58
    preparing image files, 54, *54,* 55, *55*
    resources for software support, 105
    working with color, 55, *55*
    See also image files, preparing; software
concept, 90, 91, 108
continuous-tone images, 56, *56*
contrast, 5, 31, 46–47, *47,* 48, *48,* 108
cool colors, 28, *28*
copyright and intellectual property issues, 37
CorelDRAW, 57, 60, 108
counter, 34, *34,* 108
counterform, 47, 108
creative process, 19, 109
creative writing, 13, 109
Culebra Island, Puerto Rico, 25, *25*

Davidson, Carolyn, 71
Day, Ben, 101
Denali National Park, *65*
depth of field, 42, *42,* 109
Derrida, Jacques, 91–92
descender, 34, *34,* 109
descent line, 34, *34,* 109
design:
    defining within interpretative profession, 5
    interpretive plan considerations, 7–17
    "stop and stay" effectiveness of, 6
design, elements of:
    balancing with white space, 47–48, *48,* 114
    breaking the rules, 52
    color schemes, 21, *21, 26, 27, 27*
    creating contrast, 46–47, *47,* 48, *48*
    deciding on materials, 44–45
    hierarchy of text and images, 45–46, *46,*
        47, *47,* 48, *48,* 77, *77,* 110
    maintaining consistent design approaches,
        66
    organizing/aligning with grid layouts,
        48–51, *51*
    primary/attention-grabbing text or
        images, 45

secondary/supporting text and images, 46, *46*

    See also collaborative process; color/
        colors; composition; images;
        typography

Design for Communication (Resnick), 100

*Designing Interpretive Signs: Principles in
    Practice* (Moscardo, Ballantyne, and
    Hughes), 100

Design It Yourself (Lupton), 100

design process:
    asking for feedback, 23, 109
    brainstorming/generating ideas, 21, 108
    creativity and, 19
    generating production schedules, 22, 113
    organizing/conveying information, 21
    researching precedents/finding
        inspiration, 19–20, *20, 21,* 102
    right brain/left brain, 21, 108, 111, 113
    See also collaborative process

digital immigrants, 78, 109

dinosaurs, 14, *14*

direct mail:
    identifying audiences with, 9
    promoting specific events, 13

dots per inch, 54, *54*

dumb quotes, 33, *33*

Edison, Thomas, 95

Eisenman, Peter, 92

electronic newsletters, 69

Elements of Typographic Style (Bringhurst),
    101, *101*

elephants, 97, *97*

em-dashes, 33, 109

en-dashes, 33, 109

environment, finding inspiration, 20, *20, 21*

Environmental Interpretation (Ham), 6, 66,
    71, 98

environmental stewardship, design materials
    reflecting, 9

EPS (Encapsulated Post Script), 56–57, *57,*
    58, 60, 109

exhibit designers, 5, 109

exhibits:
    accessibility guidelines, 75
    audio components, 71, 75, *75*
    complementing existing landscapes, 75
    creating effective messages, ix, 71, 74
    maintenance of, 74, *74*
    materials and fabrications, 71, *72, 73,* 74
    as nonpersonal/"passive" interpretation, 4
    "stop and stay" effectiveness of, 6
    studies on effectiveness of, 6
    targeting specific audiences, 8, *8,* 9, *9*
    working with design/fabrication
        contractors, 71, 74

*The Experience Economy: Work is Theatre
    & Every Business a Stage* (Pine and
    Gilmore), 104

Eye on Nature, 69

Fall Creek Falls State Park, 2

feedback, 23, 109

flats, 77, *77,* 110

Flesch scale, 16

Florida, butterfly ballot design, *94*

flush left/ragged right alignment, 35, 110

flush right/ragged left alignment, 35, 110

flyers, 77, *77,* 110

focal point, 39, *39,* 110

fonts, 29, *29,* 30, *30,* 104, 110

food service, as nonpersonal/"passive"
    interpretation, 4

Forest Stewardship Council (FSC), 102

fossil fuels, 14, *14*

found objects, 43, *43,* 110

Fox Index, 16

front-line interpretation, 5

GIF (Graphic Interchange Format), 58, *58,*
    110

Gilmore, James H., 104

GIMP (GNU Image Manipulation Program),
    56, 57, 60, 110

Gladwell, Malcolm, 104

Governor Mike Huckabee Delta Rivers
    Nature Center, *79*

gradation, 5

Grand Canyon, 11

graphic artists, ix, 110

graphic design:
    meaningful design decisions, 1, 110
    resources, 100

Graphic Design Cookbook (Koren), 100

graphic designers, 5, 110

graphic design standards, 66, 113

grayscale images, 55, *55,* 110

Greenough, Horatio, 13

green supplies and materials, 102

grid layouts:
    columns/vertical guidelines, 50, 51, *51,*
        109
    five-column format, 49–51, *51*
    hanging from Axis A, Axis B and Axis C,
        50, *51*
    horizontal guidelines, 50–51, *51,* 110
    margins, 49, *49,* 50, 112
    organizing/aligning design elements,
        48–51, *51,* 110

Grid Systems in Graphic Design (Müller-
    Brockman), 49, 101

Gross, Michael, 46, 71, 75, 100, *100*

guided tours, as personal interpretation, 3

Ham, Sam, 6, 66, 71, 98

Hamarikyu Garden, Tokyo, *53*

harmony, 5

horizontal axes, 50–51, *51,* 110

"Horsepower on the Hoof," *12*

"Horsepower Under the Hood," *12*

HTML editors, 60, 110

hue, 28, 110

Hughes, Karen, 100

hyphens, 33, 110

illustrations:
    as high-end drawn images, 44, *44,* 56,
        57, 110
    software options, 60
    as vector-based images, 56, *57*

illustrators, 5, 44, 111

image files, preparing:
    CMYK color mode, 55, *55,* 108
    color on computer, 55, *55*
    compressing, 57, 58

dots per inch, 54, *54*

EPS (Encapsulated Post Script), 56, 56–57,
    58, 60, 109

file formats for print purposes, 56, *56,*
    57, *57*

GIF (Graphic Interchange Format), 58,
    58, 110

GIMP (GNU Image Manipulation
    Program), 56, 57, 60, 110

grayscale images, 55, *55,* 110

JPEG/JPG (Joint Photographic Experts
    Group), 57, 58, 111

Pantone Matching System (PMS), 55, 112

pixel-based images, 56, *56,* 113

pixels per inch, 54, *54*

PNG (Portable Network Graphics), 58

for print media, 54, *54,* 55, *55,* 56, *56,* 57,
    57

resolution, 54, *54,* 55, *55,* 113

RGB color mode, 55, *55,* 57, 113

screen or projected media files, 57–58, *58*

TIFF (Targeted Image File Format), 56, *56,*
    57, 58, 114

vector-based images, 56–57, *57,* 60, 114

images:
    aligning in grid layout, 51, *51*
    alternatives to clip art, 43, *43,* 44
    composing attractive images, 37–38, *38,* 39
    copyright and intellectual property issues,
        37
    creating angles and perspective, 41, *41*
    of found objects, 43, *43,* 110
    hierarchy of text and images, 45–46, *46,*
        47, *47,* 48, *48,* 77, *77,* 110
    illustrations, 43, 44, *44,* 110, 111
    leading viewer's eye into frame, 41, *41*
    online resources, 103
    photo retouching and image manipulation
        software, 59, *59,* 60
    See also photographs/photography

iMovie, 61, 111

Information Design (Kealy), 79

Interaction of Color (Albers), 102, *102*

International Typographic Style, 49, 111

Internet:
    designing and building websites, 60–61,
        78, *78,* 79
    online interpretation and design
        resources, 103–104

interpersonal skills, 87, 111

interpretation:
    as an art, 4
    approaches for children, 4
    budgets and staffing, 2
    defining, 3, 111
    as mission-based, 9, 98
    nonpersonal, 3–4, 112
    personal/active, 3, 6, 113
    as persuasive communication to specific
        audiences, 4
    presenting whole rather than phase, 4
    as provocation, 4
    resources, 98, *98,* 99, *99*
    spoken and written word training, ix
    Tilden's principles of, 4
    visual aids and audio-visual features,
        66–67, *67,* 68, 71, 75, *75*
    See also nonpersonal media

Interpretation for the 21st Century (Beck and Cable), 5, 78, 99
Interpreting for Park Visitors (Lewis), 79
Interpreting Our Heritage (Tilden), 4, 5, 99, *99*
Interpretive Planning (Brochu), 5, 7, 99
interpretive plans/interpretive planning:
    choosing an interpretive medium, 13, 74
    defining, 7–8, 111
    design considerations and, 7–17
    developing themes, subthemes, and
        storylines, *10, 11, 11,* 12, *12,* 74,
        108, 114
    elements of, 7–17
    establishing a purpose and objectives,
        9–10, *10*
    goals of media selection, 6
    interpretive writing in media, 13–14
    outlining design considerations, 7
    resource implications, 10
    understanding the audience, 8, *8,* 9, *9*
interpretive writing:
    avoiding jargon, *14,* 15, 111
    brevity and conciseness, *14,* 15, 69–70
    consistent newsletters, 69–70
    copy-editing, 17, *17*
    features/characteristics of, 13–15, 111
    following rules of grammar, 16
    keeping it simple, 15–16
    measuring readability, 5, 15–16
    multilingual text and space, 16, *16*
    readers/audiences, 5, 16
    timeless or pop phrases, 17
Interpretive Writing (Leftridge), 15, *98,* 99

jargon, *14,* 15, 111
Jobs, Steve, 91
journalism, 13, 111
JPEG/JPG (Joint Photographic Experts
    Group), 57, 58, 111
justified typographic alignment, 35, 111

Kealy, Meagan, 79
kerning, 32, 111
Keynote, 61
kiosks, matching themes with target
    audiences, 13
Knight, Phil, 71
Koren, Leonard, 100
Krause, Jim, 69, 76, 77

Lake Chuzenji, *55*
Layout Index (Krause), 69, 76, 77
leading, 32, *32,* 51, 111
leatherback turtles, 25, *25*
Left Brain, 21, 108, 111
Leftridge, Alan, 15, *98,* 99
letterform, parts of, 34, *34,* 107
Lewis, Shea, 1, 2
Lewis, William, 79
Logo Design (Pedersen, ed.), 102
Logo Lounge, 102
logos:
    creating, 70–71
    history of NAI logo(s), 70
    resources for developing, 102
    software options, 60
    as vector-based images, 56–57, *57,* 111
Lupton, Ellen, 100

Management of Interpretive Sites (Merriman
    and Brochu), 71, 99
maps:
    ease in reading, 79, *79,* 80, 112
    orienting to reality*,* 79
    portability, 13
margins, 49, *49,* 50, 110
mean line, 34, *34,* 112
media:
    defining, 112
    developing message matrix, 11, *11*
    See also nonpersonal media
"Meeting in the Middle: Combining
    Elements of Interpretation and
    Graphic Design," 1
Meggs, Philip B., 101
membership, evaluating for target audiences, 8
Merriman, Tim, 71, 99
message element, 112
Microsoft Expression Web, 61, 112
Microsoft Publisher, 59, 112
Mills, Enos, 4–5, 99
monochromatic colors, 27, *27,* 112
monospaced font, 33, 112
Monterey Bay Aquarium, *7, 9*
Moscardo, Gianna, 100
Muir Woods National Monument, 40, *40*
Müller-Brockman, Josef, 49, 101
multimedia and video software, 61
multi-sensory experience, 112
MyFonts, 104

National Association for Interpretation
    (NAI):
    Certified Heritage Interpreter program, 2
    defining interpretation, 3
    Green Pages directory, 15, 44, 85
    history of NAI logo(s), 70
    International Conferences, 1–2, 36, *37*
    Legacy Trust Fund campaign, 43, *43*
    mission and resources, 98, *98*
    National Workshops, 1, 36, *36*
National Association of Photoshop
    Professionals (NAPP), 60, 105
National Center on Accessibility (NCA), 75
National Parks Conservation Association
    (NPCA), 84
National Park Service (NPS):
    Graphic Identity Program, 89, *89*
    Information Design training manual, 66
    online images, 103
    statistics on effectiveness of nonpersonal
        media, 6
    studies of communication skills of park
        rangers, 4
negative space/white space, 47–48, *48,* 114
neutral colors, 28, 112
newsletters, 69, *69,* 70, 112
Newton, Isaac, 26, 109
Nike swoosh, 71
The Non-Designer's Design Book (Williams),
    100
nonpersonal interpretation, 3–4, 112
nonpersonal media:
    effectiveness of, 6
    graphic design decisions for, 2, 5
    interpretive forms of, 3–4
    quality of, 5–6

software for creating, 59, *59,* 60–61
nonrenewable resources, 14, *14*

Olympic National Park, *21*
orphans, 31, 112

paragraph alignment, types of, 35
Parkin Archeological State Park, 1, *75*
"passive" interpretation, 3–4
PDF (Portable Document Format), 59, 60,
    112
Peabody Natural History Museum, 6
personal interpretation, 3, 6, 113
Personal Interpretation (Merriman and
    Brochu), 99, 99
photographs/photography:
    aligning in grid layout, 51, *51*
    books as permanent mementos, 80
    composing attractive images, 37–38, *38,* 39
    creating angles and perspective, 41, *41*
    cropping techniques, 40, *40*
    depth of field, 42, *42,* 109
    digital photography technology, 36
    of found objects, 43, *43,* 110
    indirect light/avoiding automatic flash, 43
    leading viewer's eye into image, 39, *39,* 41,
        41, 110
    photo retouching and image manipulation
        software, 59, *59,* 60
    rule of thirds and/or fifths, 38, *38,* 113
    single-lens reflex (SLR) cameras, 42, 113
    sources of, 36–37, 103, *103,* 114
    stock photography, 37, 103, *103,* 114
    sunlight and shadows, 39, *39,* 42, *42*
    textures of nature, 40, *40*
    visual identity/color scheme of, 36, *36,*
        37, 114
Pine, Joseph II, 104
pixel-based images, 56, *56,* 113
pixels per inch, 54, *54*
PNG (Portable Network Graphics), 58
polar bears, 11
Powerpoint/Microsoft PowerPoint:
    advantages and disadvantages of, 67, 68
    creating good slides, 67, *67*
    maintaining interpretive principles with,
        68
    presentations using, 61, 66–67, *67,* 68, 112
primary colors, 26, *26,* 113
Print, 102
printers and fabricators:
    providing specifications/design
        guidelines, 63, 84, 89, 113
    soliciting bids, 62–63
    touring facilities, *62*
proportion, 5
publications:
    graphic design standards/site publication
        plan, 66, 113
    as nonpersonal/"passive" interpretation, 4
Puerto Morelos, Mexico, *39*

QuarkXPress, 59, 113

Red Rock Canyon, 42, *42*
repetition, 5
Resnick, Elizabeth, 100
reversed-out type, 113

RGB color mode, 55, *55*, 57, 113
Right Brain, 21, 108, 113
Robin Williams Design Workshop (Williams and Tollett), 100
Rocky Mountain National Park, 4–5, 41, *41*
Route 66, 36, *36*
rule of fifths, 38, *38*
rule of thirds, 38, *38*, 113

sans serifs, 29, *29*, 113
saturation of color, 28, 113
secondary colors, 26, *26*, 113
senior citizens, identifying target audiences, 9
sepia tones, 26
serif, 29, *29*, 34, *34*, 113
shade, 28, 113
signatures, 49–50, 63, 113
signs:
    accessibility guidelines, 75
    audio components, 71, 75, *75*
    complementing existing landscapes, 75
    creating effective messages, 71, 74
    maintenance of, 74, *74*
    materials and fabrications, 71, *72*, *73*, 74
    as nonpersonal/"passive" interpretation, 4
    resources for designing, 100
    3-30-3 Rule, 46
    working with design/fabrication contractors, 63, 71, 74
Signs, Trails, and Wayside Exhibits (Gross, Zimmerman, and Buchholz), 46, 71, 75, 100, *100*
single-lens reflex (SLR) cameras, 42, 113
site publications plans, 66, 113
smart quotes, 33, *33*
software:
    designing and building websites, 60–61, 78, *78*, 79
    logo designs/illustrations, 60
    multimedia and video, 61
    PDF (Portable Document Format), 59, 60, 112
    photo retouching and image manipulation software, 59, *59*, 60
    plug-in applications, 113
    publication and page layout, 59
    resources and support, 105
    See also image files, preparing; computers
specifications, 63, 84, 89, 113
Sperry, Roger W., 21, 108
stem, 34, *34*, 114
Stilgoe, John, 20
stock photography, 37, 103, *103*, 114
Stroh/Dickens Barn Exhibits, 12, *12*
student audiences, cognitive objectives of, 10, *10*
surveys, evaluating for target audiences, 8

Tacoma Glass Museum, *19*
target markets, 8
technical specifications:
    online resources, 105
    preparing image files, 54, *54*, 55, *55*, 56, *56*, 57, *57*, 58
    pre-press to production, 53
    software associated with nonpersonal media, 59, *59*, 60–61

technical writing, 13, 114
templates, 67, *67*, 68, 114
tertiary colors, *26*, 27, 114
Texas Parks and Wildlife Department, *69*
themes:
    central themes, *10*, 11, *11*, 12, *12*, 108
    defining, 11, 12, *12*, 114
    developing subthemes/storylines, 11, *11*, 12, *12*
    effective nonpersonal media, 6
TIFF (Targeted Image File Format), 56, *56*, 57, 58, 114
Tilden, Freeman:
    as "father of interpretation," 4, *4*
    on interpretive treatment of content, ix, 69
    principles of interpretation, 4, 99
tint, 28, 114
tourists, identifying target audiences, 9
Trendhunter.com, 104
TrendWatching, 104
typefaces:
    affecting overall message, 6, 10
    selecting, 29, *29*, 30, *30*, 103
    See also typography
Type in Motion (Woolman), 101
Type in Motion 2 (Woolman), 101
Typographic Design: Form and Communication (Carter, Day, and Meggs), 101
typography:
    alignment of text, 35
    animated, 101
    avoiding widows and orphans, 31, 112, 114
    basic rules of, 30–35
    centered text, 35, 108
    creating contrast, 31
    decorative fonts, 29, *29*, 30, *30*, 109
    em-dashes, en-dashes, and hyphens, 33, 109, 110
    expressive qualities of, 30
    justified alignment, 35, 111
    kerning, 32, 111
    letterform, parts of, 34, *34*, 107
    letter spacing, 32, *32*, 111
    line spacing, 32, *32*
    maintaining integrity of type, 31, *31*
    maximizing legibility, 30
    paragraph alignments, 35
    pluralizing without apostrophes, 35
    point size and leading, 32, *32*, 51, 111
    resources, 101
    sans serifs, 29, *29*, 113
    selecting typefaces, 29, *29*, 30, *30*, 31
    serifs, 29, *29*, 34, *34*, 113
    single-space after punctuation, 32–33
    smart quotes vs. dumb quotes, 33, *33*
    typeface vs. font, 29, *29*, 30, *30*, 110, 114
    upper-and lower-case letters, 31

Vancouver, 36, *37*
Vancouver Aquarium, *27*
vector-based images, 56–57, *57*, 60, 114
visual identity, 36, *36*, *37*, 114
Volkswagen Beetle advertisement, 48, *48*

Warhol, Andy, 91
warm colors, 28, *28*, 114

wayside exhibits:
    accessibility guidelines, 75
    audio components, 71, 75, *75*
    complementing existing landscapes, 75
    creating effective messages, 71, 74, 114
    maintenance of, 74, *74*
    matching themes with target audiences, *11*, 13
    materials/fabrications, 71, *72*, *73*, 74
    3-30-3 Rule, 46
    working with design/fabrication contractors, 71, 74
Webmonkey.com, 102
websites:
    color palette of, 78
    designing and building, 60–61, 78, *78*, 79
    digital immigrants and, 78, 109
    as first contact, 5–6
    as Internet-based resources, 5–6, 114
    interpretive messages in, ix
    navigation of, 78–79
    reading patterns of, 78, *78*
    referencing important themes, 13
    targeting specific audiences of, 8, *8*, 9, *9*
    updating and keeping current, 78–79
    viewing in different browsers, 78–79
white space/negative space, 47–48, *48*, 114
widows, 31, 114
Williams, Robin, 100
Windows Movie Maker, 61, 114
Woolman, Matthew, 101
writing:
    creative writing, 13, 109
    interpretive writing, 13–15, 111
    journalism, 13, 111
    technical writing, 13, 114

X-Height, 34, *34*, 114

Zimmerman, Ron, 46, 71, 75, 100, *100*
Zion National Park, 40, *40*